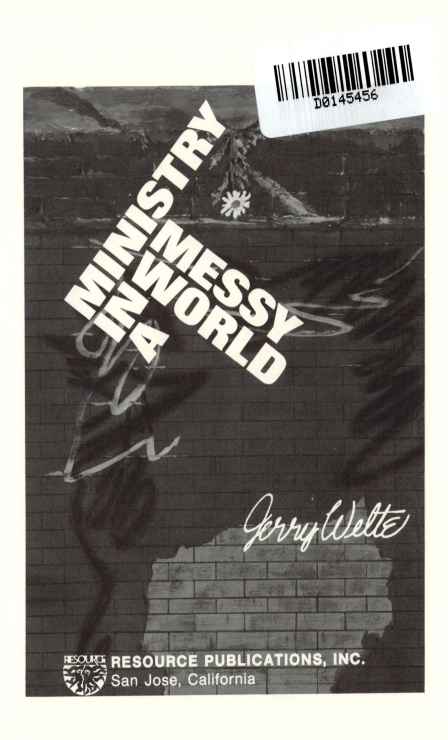

MINISTRY IN A MESSY WORLD

Jerry Welte

RESOURCE PUBLICATIONS, INC.
San Jose, California

Editorial director: Kenneth Guentert
Production editor: Elizabeth J. Asborno
Art director: Terri Ysseldyke-All
Cover design: Jean Snow
Editorial assistant: Michelle Moreland

Reprint Department
Resource Publications, Inc.
160 E. Virginia Street, Suite 290
San Jose, CA 95112-5848

Library of Congress Cataloging in Publication Data available
ISBN 0-89390-154-7
5 4 3 2 1 / 93 92 91 90 89

For my mother, Rita Welte,
For mothers everywhere,
Who teach us all the heart of ministry:
Not to abandon God's children
When they get in a mess.

Contents

Acknowledgments

Publishing any book is first and foremost a work of dependency; it is a product of community. I would like to express my gratitude to all those who have formed the community of my life, whose stories have unfolded as part of mine and revealed whatever truth these pages hold.

Secondly, I owe a great debt of gratitude to those who have responded to this project with enthusiasm, suggestions, encouragement, and criticism. Their support has brought this work to fruition. Special thanks are due to Joan Kennedy for her generous work as proofreader.

This book draws upon the wisdom found in the midst of what is often termed "secular" society in the form of plays, films, and books. I thank these artists for their testimony to the Incarnate Spirit of God and encourage the reader to take advantage of the works cited here in their entirety. I also thank the authors of other pastoral works quoted within for their contributions to this book's message.

I thank my wife, Marlene, for her excitement and commitment to the book, especially through the inspiration of her life dedicated to growth even in messy circumstances. I thank my stepchildren, Eric and Mark, for their patience during my many retreats to what they have termed "the cave" to write this book.

Finally, I thank my editor, Ken Guentert, for his support and guidance. He has been a pleasure to work with.

Introduction

"I don't think we're in Kansas anymore, Toto."
Frank L. Baum: *The Wizard of Oz*

"You must be perfect, just as your Father in heaven is perfect" (Matt 5/48). I suggest that few words in Scripture have been taken to heart by the Church as fully as these. Indeed, while we may give other passages more attention in our speaking and writing, this call to perfection has dominated our existence, driven our imaginations, and characterized our ministry as much as any other Biblical mandate.

I am well-suited to recognize this drive and comment upon its consequences, for I am a perfectionist from the word "go," a number one within the Enneagram system of personality analysis. As such an idealist, offering a kind of editorial upon perfectionism in the life and

1

ministry of the Church, I can begin by announcing some good news and some bad news. The good news is that a thirst for flawlessness is usually supported by the energy to overcome obstacles in the drive toward excellence. The bad news is the co- existence of an equal adeptness at finding the glitch in any accomplishment, no matter how carefully conceived or executed.

While many people find consolation in the words: "every cloud has a silver lining," a perfectionist is haunted daily by the realization that "every silver lining has a cloud." So, while my nature has enabled me to design some refined programs, it has often left me alone afterwards to ponder the hidden flaw. The words which haunt the perfectionist in the lonely late hours are "if only...": If only I had done this or thought of that, the experience would have been perfect. Such is the blessing and the curse of the search for perfection. One part of me engages messy reality in an effort to make it livable (call it home), while my "other self" fights tooth and nail with life, refusing to acknowledge its "impurities." Gradually, experience has revealed that the very creativity which allows me to bring beauty out of chaos would be impossible if I were predominantly an organizer, more orderly and in control while less messy. In part, this book chronicles the faith journey which has led to that conversion.

But this book is not about an individual, it is about a community. Yet, an historical predilection for identifying the Church as an institution immediately defines our problem. It is the very nature of an institutional Church to organize. Accordingly, this

Church is being true to herself, doing her job, when engaged in "straightening up" the world. Of course, the presupposition of this activity is that it clears the way for the coming of the savior: "In the desert prepare the way of the Lord; make straight in the wasteland a highway for our God!" Notice that we are called to "straighten up" the path the Lord takes. It is out of this conviction that the Lord prefers straight paths that we have invested ourselves so heavily in the drive for perfection.

This quest has manifested itself in all manner of attitudes and actions in the history of the Church. Human finitude was long disdained as the jealous rival of divine infinity. Our expressions of sorrow for sin were flawed, but they bore repeating in the hope that one day we would manage a "perfect act of contrition." We were always happy to gain an indulgence, but ecstatic to merit a plenary indulgence. Though marginal acceptance was ours as long as we kept the big blotches off our souls (mortal sins), we were never quite at ease because of all those little stains (venial sins). A "low Mass" was nice, but a "high Mass" was better, and a "solemn high Mass" was glorious! It was fine to receive communion from the priest, but how much greater if I got the pastor: "How can they expect me to receive from just an ordinary lay person?!"

Yet, the Church is by no means alone in this discontent with the limitations of life. The society we live in, with all its ambiguity and stress, is straining to build some sense of stability and order into its existence. It is no coincidence that musicals and westerns no longer grace our movie screens. Their death symbolizes

3

something that has died in us. We grew up on "Dick
Van Dyke," "Dragnet," and "Combat." Our children
are being raised on "Kate And Allie," "Hill Street
Blues," and "television wars" like Vietnam. All of our
science and technology, our corporations and
legislatures, our psychology and medicine have not been
able to sort out the jumble of contemporary existence.
Life is still very messy indeed and there does not seem
to be an easy way out of the wilderness.

So, since our efforts to duel with reality have not yet
"tamed the beast," we have resorted to escape
measures which we hope will provide some sense of law
and order, or at least allow us to forget the mess for a
while. These means reveal the depth of our passion for
perfection, the extremes to which we are willing to go in
order to "be perfect," regardless of the illusory quality
of our various definitions of perfection.

Growing drug and alcohol use reveals how even a
temporary escape from a messy world is worth the price
of creating another, more serious dilemma. Rambo is
popular at the movies because he makes a very messy
war neat, showing us exactly who the bad guys are and
winning a lost cause in a few hours. "Wheel of
Fortune's" Vanna White is not America's dream girl
because she challenges us to appreciate the mystery and
fullness of womanhood, but because she is never seen in
curlers, always does her chores with a smile, and never
asks for conversation or to be taken out to dinner. The
Huxtables are America's favorite family, not for
addressing complex racial and domestic issues, but
because they are cute, solve their problems in thirty

minutes, and pull down about eighty grand a year in TV salary. Even our national pastime is dedicated enough to neatness to appoint a "cleanup hitter" when the bases are loaded with runners.

All these cultural flights of fantasy are effective signs of the tenacity of our desire to be perfect, to escape the messiness and ambiguity of life. If we reflect upon our experience well enough, however, we are drawn to the conclusion that such flawlessness is an illusion, that messiness is inevitable. But even if we do not pay attention, the stone wall of everyday life will eventually lead us to ask some hard questions about our presuppositions or necessitate drastic measures to stave those questions off. Everyday living, though, is unyielding in its message: "Life is messy."

I recall a conversation I had with my brother while he was pastor of a midwestern parish. He related two stories which tragically confirm this conviction:

1. A fourth grader walked home from school one evening, took out a gun, went to his room, and shot himself. He had left a note for his parents and had also indicated in some fashion to a few of his classmates in school that day that he "would not be around much longer." The parents and children were left to deal with their tragic loss as well as all the "if only..." questions that accompany our desire to make things all-right.

2. A teenage couple went out on a date. The boy drank heavily and was drunk when he drove the girl home. When the accident occurred the girl was thrown through the windshield and killed, while the boy walked

away with hardly a scratch. Again, those left behind were given the lot of sorting out the ambiguity and injustice of such an event.

Such stories need not isolate us, but can draw us together in the solidarity of the mess, for there is no escape from such experiences in life for any of us. The only choice we own is the option to face them and change or to deny them and seek escape. In many ways we have not paid enough attention to these experiences. We have not been honest about them and we have not paid heed to their wisdom for the welfare of the human community and the development of Church ministry.

About This Book

This work is about ministry, but while geared mainly toward professional or formal ministry, it also touches upon the kind of caring we engage in with one another each day: the ministry of a father to his son, a teacher to her student, a priest to his parishioner, a wife to her spouse. More to the point, however, it is about ministry in the mess: the care of a father for his gay son, a teacher for her abused student, a priest for his divorced parishioner, a wife for her alcoholic spouse.

While the stories told here will emphasize the messiness and ambiguity of life, it is certainly not my intention to canonize disorder or to minimize divine power and life's wonder. We all have our tales of "amazing grace" and revelation (Transfiguration), and those stories need to be told. Yet, in the end we must "come down from the mountain" despite our preference for erecting tents and "staying on top." It would be understandable to be put off by the use of the word "mess" to describe a faith experience of human existence. In fact, this is the sort of book that might lend itself to the familiar contemporary criticism of being humanistic (secular humanism) in a way that subordinates the transcendant element of religious experience. The reader will find here a highly experiential reflection intended to underscore the human side of the divine/human partnership that makes ministry work. Its experiential bias is properly balanced by works that emphasize the transcendant while employing more scholastic or metaphysical language.

This book is divided into two parts. The first section deals primarily with defining the mess, identifying the sort of existence we live. This requires looking at life's dark side and related historical perceptions of God with the reflective stance needed to learn from them. If this seems at times to be pessimistic, it is only to compensate for a temptation born of piety which seeks to gloss over the mess and find escape.

Once we have taken an honest look at experience and that look has discovered the mess, we can begin to consider the implications of human ambiguity for pastoral care: ministering in the mess. If our ministry is to help people, it must be able to meet them on the ground of their existence, even if that ground is shaky and demands more resourceful and flexible skills than we have ever cared to admit. It is my sincere hope that the pastoral journey this book invites will ring true for its readers so as to allow them to reassess and adjust their own care for others in whatever fashion is reasonable and helpful. The stories I tell at various points have been the springboards for the process of restructuring my own pastoral assumptions and strategies. They are the experiences which have allowed me to come a bit closer to being the only kind of minister I believe can truly be of help to God's people: a minister in the mess.

Who This Book Is For

This book is primarily geared toward professional ministers or pastoral teams who are seeking a tool for the re-evaluation and re-formation of ongoing ministry. While the principles discussed here would certainly be applicable to any caring relationship (parents, spouses, etc.), it is the individual or group engaged in formal ministry who would be best served by them. Here, then, are some of the most likely people or groups to benefit from this material:

1. An individual minister who is seeking a new direction and/or an evaluation of ministry. The benefits of this process might then be shared with any larger pastoral group to which the individual belongs.

2. A pastoral staff or ministry board which is responsible for setting the agenda or direction for ministry and/or ministerial formation.

3. Any ongoing ministry in the parish (catechists, social justice committee, liturgical ministers, etc.) who might use all or part of the book for reflection, formation, or goal setting.

4. A parish council, pastoral council, or similar group who might be looking to shift their agenda away from a business orientation (maintenance, finance, etc.) toward a pastoral focus.

5. A school board or religious education board seeking a foundation on which to formulate a new or base their existing approach to religious education, liturgy, sex education, AIDS curriculum, etc.

6. A group of committed, involved adults from various segments of a parish or community wishing to gather for a designated period of time (eg. a Lenten renewal program) to take a look at their faith and ministry with an eye toward renewal.

Alternative Time Frames

This book could be used in any of several time frames, depending on the needs, commitments, and availability of the group in question. Here are some possibilities:

1. Intensive Retreat/Year-End Staff Review

This option is best suited to professional staffs or teams who can set aside time for this project. Sessions would vary according to available time. A six-day experience would allow for exactly two sessions a day, one chapter per session.

A four-day period would entail covering three chapters a day.

Allowances could be made for time by dropping or combining some chapters. It should be noted that there is no inherent value in covering chapters, but only in dialoguing about the issues which the material raises for the particular group in question. From this perspective, the best approach might be to simply have everyone read the book and gather to respond to it within the pastoral context of the team. Whatever model serves the development of the group as effective ministers is the best approach to adopt.

2. One Year of Twelve Monthly Sessions

This option would be more flexible for various groups, but might be best suited for parish boards or staffs who have ongoing agenda items to consider, but could afford a monthly session (or part of one) for ongoing evaluation and renewal. Thus, all or part of one staff meeting a month or a monthly board meeting could be devoted to this work. An added benefit to this option is the convenience with which the book's twelve chapters fit into a monthly cycle.

3. Six-Week Lenten Renewal Program

This alternative might be ideal for adult renewal groups or parishioners in general who are involved in any type of ministry. The chapters can be divided into twos to be covered over the six available weeks of Lent (including Holy Week) or the sessions could start during the week of Ash Wednesday in order to avoid Holy Week. If covering all the material presents a problem, the group can select those chapters most appropriate to their interests or needs.

4. Six-Week
Adult Education/Ministerial Formation Program

This would involve a six-week commitment similar to the above (two chapters a week or selected chapters). The advantage here is that this option can be offered as one part of a year's adult education offerings. Thus, participants need only commit to this one section (ie. this would be one offering among a series of six week sessions on various topics). Parish ministries could also undergo a similar program over a suitable period during the year.

Model Session

Once again, the structure of sessions might vary greatly depending on the needs and composition of the group. Yet, my experience with using this material in a parish setting has suggested a beneficial model. The sessions would last from ninety minutes to two hours, including a break at the midpoint. Each session would procede as follows:

1. Brief opening prayer
2. Retelling of opening story (which is introduced at the end of the previous session)
3. Review of basic points of reflection (which each participant should read prior to the session)
4. Questions, clarifications, and reactions to material
5. Break
6. Working through questions for reflection/group process
7. Engaging in one or more activities (optional)
8. Closing liturgy (related to material for current session)
9. Assigning of reading for next session
10. Telling of opening story for next session

PART ONE

GETTING AWAY FROM MINISTRY AS HOUSEKEEPING

"In the beginning, when God created the heavens and the earth, the earth was a formless wasteland, and darkness covered the abyss, while a mighty wind swept over the waters."
— Genesis 1/1-2

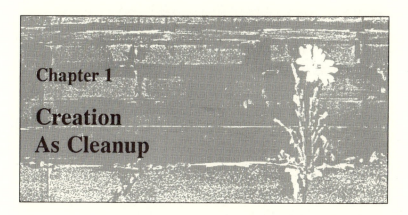

Chapter 1

Creation
As Cleanup

"And we've got to get ourselves back to the garden."
— Joni Mitchell: Woodstock

I remember having lunch with one of my closest
friends a few years ago. It was a most interesting
encounter in that we ate almost no food, although we
did order and our plates sat before us throughout the
"meal." Both of us were at crossroads in our lives,
junctures which were tearing at our relationship. These
personal circumstances limited our time together and
strained the little time we found. It was somewhere in
the midst of this turbulent period in our relationship
that she set the stage for our pivotal luncheon date by
calling me and stating the obvious: "We have to talk."

Our lunch began normally enough, but the
undercurrents of what was to come were noticeably

present. A casual observer might have likened our conversation to watching a Yellowstone ranger give tourists the scientific reasons for the phenomenon of "Old Faithful" even as steam starts to seep from the ground and the earth begins to tremble. Our words sounded calm and rational, but signs of an imminent eruption loomed about us.

So it was that our polite tones soon gave way to hurtful and angry ones as unexpressed and unresolved feelings boiled to the surface on both sides of the table. Most of our attempts to save ourselves from the full force of the confrontation through the normalcy of eating were defeated by our inability to control what was happening. Before long tears were flowing and our feelings were difficult to verbalize. We left that encounter shaken and uncertain, but having made the first tentative steps toward what was to be the eventual reconciliation of our friendship.

The Creation Myth
and Conflict Management

What happened that afternoon was the inevitable messiness that accompanies the grace of relationship whenever two lives encounter each other. The basic human activity of sharing food became the context for an outpouring of so many hurt feelings and misunderstandings that we were simply overwhelmed and incapacitated by them at the time. One strong sensation I experienced that day was a deep longing to return to a former and more simple time in my relationship with this friend, that idealistic vision we often adopt of the past as "the good old days." I remember feeling that the pain could easily have been avoided if I had done the right things ("If only I..."). I recall wishing that if we could just get by this trouble our friendship would once more return to a time of peace and harmony ("Someday soon maybe...").

All of us grapple with this gut instinct to handle our problems (messes) in one of the three ways mentioned above. In the midst of a crisis we:

1. idealize the past and long for its simplicity and neatness;

2. regret how the current state of affairs could have been avoided if we had only taken this or that perfect course of action;

3. project ourselves into a future where the present mess has been mopped up to allow a return to normalcy.

Where did we get this instinctive method of conflict management? I believe it is rooted in that ancient, most primordial of religious myths: the story of the Garden. A myth is a powerful thing. It creates entire worlds and value systems; it gives meaning to our existence and order to our beliefs. Myths, like liturgy, are both the expression and the architect of our faith. Yet, identical myths have been the foundation of contrary value systems, different faiths. This is so because, while myths are basic to all humanity, their interpretation is specific to human subgroups: tribes, nations, religious sects, etc.

To comprehend the workings of a myth within a particular society or group, we must study more than the story itself; we must question how it has been understood and developed by those employing it.

We can be sure that almost every culture and religion has some sort of creation myth. Yet, the formulation and retelling of that tale within each particular culture or religion reveals as much about the culture as it does about the reality of creation or the God who creates. The creation myth indigenous to Christianity is found in Genesis and is rooted in the symbol of the Garden. How has the story of creation been understood in the development of the Christian tradition? How has the symbol of the Garden been interpreted? In order to more fully understand our ministry we now turn to those two vital questions.

The Christian sense of the creation myth can be stated so simply and directly that it is easy to miss its implications for the shaping of our pastoral practice over the centuries. While a scholar may state this myth in much more technical ways, most Christians have engrained in them that the basic truth of our existence goes something like this:

1. There was a big mess (chaos)
2. God straightened everything up (creation)
3. People made a big mess again (Original Sin)
4. With God's help we've got to get our mess cleaned up (Redemption).

I believe this to be an accurate summary of the way
the Garden story was rendered while I was growing up
Catholic in the fifties. Out of several possible
interpretations of the creation myth, many Christians
have adopted this one. The primal world was one of
incredible chaos, unbelievable messiness. Then along
came our hero, God, to demonstrate supreme power by
cleaning it all up, restoring order, and creating the
perfect world of the Garden. This unblemished
existence was graciously offered to us, God's people.
We had a chance to live in a perfect place, a spotless
utopia. Yet, fools that we are, we blew it. We made a
mess by committing Original Sin. Since that time, the
primary purpose of human existence can be summed up
in one activity: cleaning up our mess to get back into
"God's good graces."

Catholic Schools As Models
of Housekeeping Ministry

Our reading of the creation myth, our interpretation
of the symbol of the Garden, gave birth to what I would
call "the housekeeping model" of Christian ministry.
This model presumes that the dream which captures our
imaginations and the call which inspires our efforts is
the enterprise of tidying up or keeping house. Such a
goal translates into a ministry founded upon law and
order, perfection and neatness, simplicity and

spotlessness. This ministry can be capsulized in the image which describes "the human race" as a relentless marathon to "get back to the Garden."

If there is any doubt that the housekeeping mentality has grown into a dominant force in our ministerial imaginations, we need only reflect upon our private and communal experience of growing up Christian, especially as reflected in the world of the Catholic grammar school (other denominations would do well to reflect upon their Christian educational roots). In examining these basic Christian experiences, we do not mean to condemn them out of context, but to consider them in terms of contemporary insights and needs in ministry. If the current Christian adult population is heavily influenced by the housekeeping model in their ministry, it is surely in part because they have learned to be spiritual housekeepers from their youth.

The preoccupation with maintaining discipline and order in the parochial school system of the 50's makes it a symbol of the type of pastoral "schooling" in which the present generation of adult ministers discover their roots and priorities. It is the changing presuppositions of ministry in our time that raise the question of our need to "go back to school." Consider the number of activities in a Catholic school that were designed to train us to be neat and orderly while providing for a smooth and efficient atmosphere within the school itself. How many times a day were we told to "get in line?" Indeed, anyone who could not learn to "stay in line" had a rough time making it in a Catholic school. How many of the day's activities were initiated or concluded with a bell? The entire day was neatly parcelled out by these bells which most often told us once again to get in line. How many times a year were we asked to clean out or straighten our desks?

In a Catholic school there was no behavior more rewarded or reinforced than orderly behavior. No action was more punished than an unruly one. The penalty for such messy activity was often symbolic of the crime. The offender was made to sit away from the group, exiled from the neat rows of desks, often in a corner where straight lines collide and dust collects. In the school I attended the principal owned three rulers of varying size and weight, one to match the relative severity of each disorderly act. The Catholic school system produced people with character and many people who were characters, but it graduated very few people who could honestly claim: "I don't do windows." Catholic schools taught people how to "clean up their act" in every sense of the phrase.

Creation and Ministry: A Matter of Time

This preoccupation with law and order might be traced back to many possible sources in the history of the church. Yet, one of its roots must certainly be acknowledged as our reading of the Genesis creation myth, our interpretation of the symbol of the Garden. More specifically, the housekeeping model of ministry is rooted in the order in which we relate the events of the creation myth, the sense of time we utilize in our reading of that story. We have learned to tell the account of creation with a sense of chronological time (a Greek/Western notion of time as linear, events as sequential) rather than personal time (a Hebrew notion of time as a personal whole and temporal events as interrelated within that whole).

In simple terms this means that the housekeeping model of ministry is a natural outgrowth of a chronological reading of the creation myth. If first there was a mess, then God brought order, then we messed it all up, the next logical step is for us to restore lost order by wiping up the mess we made. If Original Sin is not in a true sense "original" (primordial), but appears subsequent to the complete order and beauty of the garden, then authentic ministry is naturally geared toward getting back to the first, unblemished state of things. In this scenario the Garden is a symbol of a state of affairs which was lost, but can be rescued through the concerted efforts of a housekeeping ministry.

What happens to our ministerial model, however, if we read the creation myth with a sense of personal time, of the significance of various events relative to one another rather than in terms of chronological order? Through such eyes we see that sin (chaos) and creation (order) are not mutually exclusive, one following after or giving way to the other, but actually coexist in relation to one another. Each component of the creation story expresses a part of human experience that is both undeniable and inescapable.

The beauty and order of creation is told first, not because it precludes chaos or exists independently of it, but because order more appropriately symbolizes the power of God which is primary in the heart of the writer and central to the overall point of the story. The messy consequences of sin follow the introduction of order, not because they were initially absent, at least as human potential, but because the meaning of sin simply cannot be communicated except in relationship to order or beauty. In the old westerns the arrival of the bad guys in town and the subsequent restoration of order by the sheriff would hardly be significant unless we first had some sense of the tranquil and productive life of the townspeople. When we read the creation myth with this sense of personal time, the Garden is a symbol of a state of affairs which is possible despite the constant coexistence of chaos in our lives. Good wins out over evil and despite evil, not after it or without it. Ministry evokes a constant creative potential, not a maintenance/repair contract.

We will look further into the implications of this view for church ministry. For now it is only necessary to see that housekeeping ministry begins with the supposition that chaos and order are mutually exclusive states of affairs which follow each other chronologically in time. The question we address here is whether contemporary ministry must begin with a reading of the creation myth which allows for the simultaneous presence of good and evil, order and chaos, and a positive sense of their interrelationship.

The three "temptations" I experienced in trying to sort out a friendship crisis over a seemingly innocent lunch are closely related to the dynamics of housekeeping ministry. My first thought was to return to an idealized past where our friendship was strong and unthreatened. Don't most of us occasionally view the church's past through rose colored glasses, longing for its comforting sense of order and simplicity? Next, I examined all the mistakes that had led to the current crisis and dredged up all the "if only's..." which might have averted it. Isn't there a fatal attraction to passing the hours bemoaning the world's sinfulness and our personal shortcomings in an effort to redeem the past and fantasize a more orderly present? Finally, I projected myself into a glorious future where the pain of the moment would be over and my friendship would once more be vibrant. Don't we find strange comfort in rationalizing our inaction on the crises of this life, telling ourselves or others that "things will work out" or "one day we will be happy in heaven"?

It is my belief that the housekeeping model of ministry is inadequate for the present day and, in fact, distracts us from the current pastoral needs of God's people. It is not my desire to form a peaceful coexistence with the mess, implying that sin is little more than inconvenient untidyness, nor to put down any efforts at bringing greater order into life. It is more my hope to suggest a basis for ministry that is more honest and consistent with the daily human experiences of the people to whom we minister. At this early juncture in that enterprise it is my aim to share a conviction which I believe is a touchstone for authentic ministry: Life is both holy (whole) and messy (broken), and ministry cannot take place anywhere else but in that graceful chaos. It does not occur before or after, without or around the messiness of life, but right in the thick of it.

AIDS:
Symbol of a New Age in Ministry

The rise of the deadly disease of AIDS has ushered in a new era in pastoral care, the age of ministry in a messy world. AIDS is a symbol of our lost pastoral innocence, of our inability to return to simpler, more idyllic times. First, this illness shatters our pragmatic approach to ministry by rendering the usual criteria for success (tangible results) ambiguous or frustrating. AIDS makes us look with increasing seriousness at that style of ministry which emphasizes abiding presence over utilitarian progress, graceful "failure" over self-gratifying success.

Next, because of its ties to homosexuality, promiscuity, and drugs, AIDS starkly defines the dilemma of a modern church caught between the calls of compassion and morality. The dying may be visited with compassion, the sinner may be called to conversion, but what are the priorities of today's minister in assisting people who are "dying of their sin"? I imply no moral stance here, but seek to place the dilemma of the modern minister in its actual context: current church teaching which defines the boundaries of pastoral practice. In the past this dilemma was more subtle because its consequences were less visible. Ministry to the divorced "by the book," for example, may have augmented the pain of people who were secretly dying on the inside, but insensitive care to AIDS victims may add to the agony of those who are very visibly dying on the outside.

Above all, however, AIDS forces us to acknowledge the limits of pastoral ministry more than ever before. Therefore, we must find new reasons to minister and new evidence as to what exactly constitutes the "fruits of our labors." A newspaper article in the *Chicago Tribune* underscored this truth as it detailed an interview with the director of a local AIDS clinic. He described the messiness of his work: "The weariness comes from feeling that anything you do is inadequate. There's so much more to be done. There aren't the resources to do it. There isn't any cure. People will go on dying...I certainly have a sense of life being much more fragile than before. I've seen people in their twenties and thirties dying on a regular basis. I look at some of my friends and I feel like I'm waiting for a bomb to go off." This feeling of being on new, unfamiliar, and unsettling ministerial ground, the conviction that we can no longer hope to "get back to the garden," is the starting point for the reflections and suggestions which follow.

Annulment:
Symbol of an "Old Age" in Ministry

While divorce ministry may not be our greatest failure to minister effectively in this messy world, it is probably a prime symbol of our hesitation in general to move boldly into the new age of pastoral care. The Catholic marriage tribunal system is a sign of the church's propensity for lingering on the borders of the pastoral frontier in favor of the appeal of ministering in otherworldly ways, in "another world." This is so because of the rationale of the annulment process which claims to nullify a marriage through the discovery of some hidden flaw which renders the union invalid from the beginning. Thus, while the marriage was legal, it is declared null because it is not and never was sacramental. There are a number of problems with this approach. First, the implication that "there never was a marriage" seems to be a denial of reality, of the ambiguity of real situations, and of life itself. It is precisely because there was so much of a personal investment in a marriage (the relationship was so real, present, and important) that the divorce procedure can be so bitter. I witnessed my wife's pain over the years as she mourned her losses and bound her wounds from a previous marriage. Are we being creatively pastoral to such people by implying that the agony they feel is really "over nothing"?

Secondly, the declaration by the church that a broken marriage was never sacramental comes across as a denial of grace, a statement of "little faith." Is it pastoral to tell two people who have spent ten years of their lives together that they were never really married in the eyes of the church or that their life together lacked sacramentality? Practically speaking, such reasoning leaves people with a hole, a meaningless space, in their lives rather than a whole, a means of integrating painful human experience toward a new life of holiness. It also suggests the notion that grace (sacramentality) is an "all or nothing" entity ("real grace" never fails; authentic grace never comes out of failure). Is life like that? Might it be more helpful to assist people in identifying both the graceful and sinful elements of the time they have invested together, perhaps in an R.C.I.A. based format for annulment? I am aware that my wife's experience of annulment reflected few of these concerns, but came across as a legal means of tying up some loose spiritual ends.

These questions are raised only superficially here so that they may be familiar to the reader when they are expanded upon later. For now it is best to focus the impact of these thoughts toward the acceptance of a messy world over a "Garden world" as the context for ministry. Transforming pastoral care for effectiveness in this context is a task that challenges every minister in the church today. It is this enterprise to which we turn our attention in the pages ahead.

Items for Individual Reflection/Group Process

1. Recall some very messy situations you have been in. How did you respond to them? When were you tempted to find a way out (escape)? When did you meet the problem head on (engagement)? Compare the positives and negatives of each approach.

2. Does the author's interpretation of our telling of the Genesis creation account resonate with your experience? How did you hear this story as a child? What was the meaning of Original Sin within that story? How did your understanding of the elements of this story affect faith and ministry as you grew up?

3. Do you tend to be a perfectionist or a realist? How does this basic attitude influence your approach to life?; to this book? How does it shape, enhance, or limit your ministry?

4. Do you agree with the author that we have labored under the illusion that we can "get back to the Garden"? Do you think that there are still traces of this kind of thinking in our pastoral life? Is this good or bad? Do you feel "at home" in the messiness of life? Why or why not?

5. Reflect upon your experiences of Christian education while growing up. What "extracurricular lessons" did the shape of those created worlds teach you about God, self, and life? How did they bias your adult ministry positively/negatively?

6. What does the disease "AIDS" say about the state of ministry today? Does it "change the rules"? In what way? In view of such realities, is there a need for new strategies or assumptions in ministry? What might some of these be?

7. Reflect upon divorce/annulment ministry in the church. If, as McLuhan says, "the medium is the message," what is the message communicated by that ministry to divorced members of the church? How might a "new message" be communicated?

8. Why have musicals and westerns died out at the movies? What kind of image of life did they depict? What does their demise say about the way we view life in contemporary culture?; in the modern church? Is this good or bad? Explain. Do you find yourself yearning for "a good old fashioned musical"? What does your answer say about you and your ministry?

9. Reflect on the experience of "beginning again" with regard to relationships, programs, New years, etc. How is this human reality of "starting over" or "giving it another try" helpful for understanding the perspective on creation taken here?

Activities for Pastoral Staffs/Ministries

1. Trace the origin of "the world" in which you now minister. How was it created? What part did God play, what part did you play in shaping its present form? What elements of chaos and order coexist in that world? What interventions are called for on your part to continually "recreate" the wonders of that world? Concretize that call.

2. Simulate a pastoral visit to a PWA (person with AIDS). This might best be done by role-playing such a visit, breaking the staff into twos to act out this encounter. After the exercise these dyads could share their perceptions of the experience. The "minister" could express his/her intended message; the "PWA" could voice the "real message" that came through and the feelings that attended it.

3. Have each person in the group list their favorite books, plays, and films. Study their endings to see what patterns emerge as to individual and group defintions of "happy endings." How do these feelings for what constitutes a happy ending influence the ministerial style of the group?

4. Study the mission statement or goals and objectives of the staff or community. What do these suggest about pastoral priorities? Do these statements reflect a desire to "clean up" or a preference for "earthy encounters"? Consider the need to rewrite these statements to reflect actual priorities.

5. Divide your staff or team into two categories: creative types and management types. The creators tend to see possibilities and initiate designs. The managers tend to work out the details and identify problems. Realizing that no one can be stereotyped by either category, sort out the complementary and conflicting elements of this partnership for your ministry. How is working out this association creatively related to the Genesis metaphor used in this chapter?

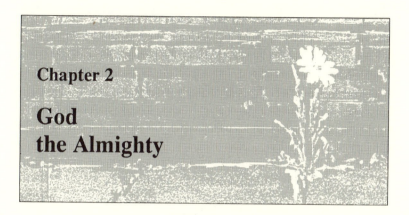

Chapter 2

God
the Almighty

"We believe in God, the Father Almighty."
— The Apostles' Creed

I remember very clearly the night I realized that I could not marry the woman to whom I was first engaged, that I would break our engagement. I awoke from a restless sleep to a decision that was at once crystal clear (unmistakably "right") and totally incomprehensible (unfathomable, cruelly wrong).

The certitude which accompanied that moment made the decision more than a choice or a desire, rather it felt like something that I "had to do." In saying this I surely do not mean to pass the buck by claiming the move was "God's will" in the same vein that some profess "the devil made me do it." I realized my own share of the blame for what was happening. The breakdown of our relationship certainly spoke of human limitation and error. Yet, it was also true that we had invested a sincerity and dedication in our love that from a faith perspective introduced the element of mystery into its failure as well. The inner processes which mediate truth for us (e.g., the truth that our marriage was not to be realized despite our hopes and efforts) sometimes come into play and identify even a destructive, mournful action as the correct one. It was this peculiar harmony/discord of divine and human wills that night which indicated the significance of the dilemma at hand for my future and that of my fiancee.

Now I suppose we all prefer to assume a stance of relative dignity in talking with God, but there was nothing dignified about my prayer that night. It was one of those prayer encounters we have all known which provides insight into the Agony of the Garden. The pain in such prayer is not rooted so much in the unpleasant task at hand, but in that violent meeting of right and wrong in the same moment. The search for another way is made desperate (agonizing) by the inner certainty that such an alternative is an illusion, even as one wildly turns over stones to find it. The "agony" in this case was not my private burden of breaking bad news, but the common suffering of two people facing the paradox of why apparently healthy relationships die, why sincere efforts fail, and why hearts in love are often broken. So, before acceding to the rightness of the call, I spent a while pleading for a way out for the two of us.

That night set the stage for a turning point in my faith journey. The events of the days that followed, the execution of my decision, led me to begin asking some of those questions upon which this book is based. I could accept the notion that my fiancee and I might be called upon to face the difficult task of letting go, as in Old Testament imagery where the people are called to "leave this land for a land which the Lord will provide." Yet, I had been raised to believe that such chores are carried out under the direction of an almighty God who, despite contrary appearances, has such situations firmly in control down to the smallest detail. This was not to prove true in this case.

The hurtfulness of the situation made it vital to choose the moment carefully for breaking the bad news. My fiancee had long planned to see London with her sister, so I determined to break our engagement shortly after her return. With a sick feeling inside I picked them up at the airport and gathered with her family to hear about the trip. In the midst of their account my fiancee and her sister looked at each other with a gleam in their eyes. They announced that they had a surprise and left the room. In a few moments they returned and my heart sank as far as my mouth must have fallen open. My fiancee was wearing a bridal hat and veil which she had purchased in London for our wedding. The joy and pride in her heart were evident in her expression. A few days later I ended our engagement and the world that we had created became only a broken dream.

Faith Meets Reality to Define Divine Power

Despite the incongruity of this clash between faith and reality, I could imagine someone reminding me that "life isn't fair" or that "God never promised you a rose garden." Such a criticism would be valid enough in isolation, but this story unfolds in the faith setting of one schooled from childhood to "believe in God, the Father almighty." In this context one might expect ill fortune or contradiction to strike at any time, but not so cruelly when responding to God's call: "We know that in all things God works for good with those who love God, those who have been called according to God's purpose" (Romans 8/28). The absurdity of the wedding hat only served to underscore the incomprehensible nature of our breakup rather than affirm its painful correctness.

This incident, then, while not changing my overall image of God overnight, certainly opened me to reflect upon past and future experiences with new biases. Such encounters with the absurd raise basic questions for the believer: "Who is God?"; "When and where will divine power be manifested?"; "How and why does the Lord make an impact upon our world?"; "Is God truly as I imagine God to be?" For our intent here, a particularly helpful way of posing such questions might be the specific query: "Is God really almighty?" or at least, "Is God almighty in the way that we have come to imagine?"

Asking such a question is by no means an isolated endeavor, but a lifetime undertaking. Each new experience provides additional data to be processed along with the existing information. Yet, the key to the process is an initial stance of openness to the question and a willingness to accept life's answers. Seemingly absurd beliefs (the earth is flat) can be safeguarded until we are willing to get into our ships and risk sailing off the edge of our world to discover vital clues toward the formulation of renewed faith.

When we make someone or something a "god," we naturally tend to idealize (idolize) that god. That idol is constructed upon an interpretation of human experience. As we continue to reflect upon that experience, the idol is either built up (worshipped) or smashed (abandoned). If we are not to lose faith in our "god" we must fit contradictory evidence into an overall pattern which allows our idealized image to survive, albeit slightly tarnished. In short, if our worship is to continue we must either explain away the questions or alter our image of this god.

This dynamic of faith was quite common in religion classes when I was growing up. We were given the ideal of a God who was almighty and for a long time we swallowed it whole because it gave us comfort and security, much like we long ate certain foods without regard to their content because they tasted so good. Then one day some smart aleck asked a question: "Can God make a rock so big that even God can't lift it?"

Although such questions were usually taken lightly, they held enough theological weight to send us back to the drawing board to rescue our image of an almighty God. While I accepted the standard answer that "God can never be self-contradictory," it hasn't stayed with me as much as the question. The answer is theological; the question is theo-imaginary. The lasting impact of this question over its answer may indicate that, although primitively stated, it was a better question than we ever cared to admit. God does, after all, make a human will so free that even God can't control it.

These questions, whether professionally worded or not, force us to make adjustments in our image of God. Even a noncontradictory God is limited in some sense of the word. It is our stories of God that generate the divine image we worship and the list of divine attributes from which we seek life and power. As those stories are challenged by experience we may cling to the old idol by ignoring or juggling the facts. On the other hand, we may yield to the birth of a "new God" who can embody old myths in a new way, who may yet be "almighty" for us in an unexpected and powerful manner.

In announcing the end of my engagement I simply could not imagine that an all powerful God would allow for the cruel and sloppy way in which "God's will" came about. Since I could not easily deny the experience, the old god had to be acknowledged as an idol and a new image of God had to be erected. In the same way many survivors of the holocaust could not continue to believe in the Yahweh of old because that God would simply never have permitted six million of the chosen people to be slaughtered. If faith in Yahweh was to continue, the image of what "Yahweh" meant had to be reformed, for the evidence of the holocaust was too big to ignore. Similarly, the patient who enters the terminal stages of cancer must come up with a new definition of "all powerful" or risk following a God who can cure at any time but chooses not to do so for inscrutable or even manipulative reasons.

Growing up provides time for looking at the evidence, examining the lived experience of the faithful, to see what valid questions it raises for the future of our image of God. Here are four possible conclusions which this process might suggest. Such conclusions are drawn from past communal experience and subject to revision based on experiences to come.

1. God Is Not Almighty (in the way we were taught)

Jesus reminded us: "As bad as you are, you know how to give good things to your children. How much more, then, will your Father in heaven give good things to those who ask him!" (Matt 7/11). If we are to continue to believe in a parent-God who will do whatever good is possible for us, the evidence of limit and loss in life leads us to the inevitable revelation that there are some things which God simply cannot do/cannot give. For shall we worship a God who can limit or remove suffering from our lives, but freely elects to allow arbitrary and unrelenting pain to afflict the poor, the helpless, and the innocent? I think not.

Consider this one possible chain of events: A lonely wife submits to the indiscretion of a brief affair. A child is inadvertently conceived and the woman's husband, hurt and angry, demands an abortion. The woman, fearing her husband's reaction will culminate in further isolation or divorce, agrees to the abortion. Her parents,

stoutly religious, are abhorred by her action and exile
her from the family circle. Overcome by guilt and
alienation, the woman takes her own life.

This is a grisly set of circumstances, but such
dominoes do fall in this life. The point of raising them at
all is theological reflection. Either God allows such
things to occur or just cannot prevent them. My
theological upbringing adopted the perspective that
God has the power to intervene in any crisis but
carefully selects when and where to do so. The benefit
of illustrating the chain of events above is the revelation
that God cannot allow one evil to occur without
implicitly giving way to the others that inevitably follow.
Just as grace has not an isolated, but a cumulative
effect, so too is evil connected. Thus, the theological
bias of this book is for the latter position. God does not
personally allow evil but, within the dynamics and limits
of this divinely chosen and created world, is powerless
to prevent it.

Does this experience of God's limits mean that we
have to alter the creed? Not at all, but it does indicate a
need to seek out a reason for the failure of divine
omnipotence. This breakdown is the result of a basic
divine attribute: benevolence. God does not hoard
power, but elects to give it away. In a world of
self-aggrandizement, the Lord is self-limiting, more
power gracious than power hungry. Once power is
shared, the Benefactor is limited by her own generosity.
For example, God cannot share with us the power of
free choice without also sacrificing the ability to prevent
us from using it destructively. Jesus reminds Pilate of

this when he is about to be condemned to death: "You would have no power over me whatever if it were not given you from above."

2. God Is Not in Control

Belief in a God of control surfaces in times of trial when our piety reassures us that "God will never send us more than we can handle." Such faith can lend itself to an image of God as expert proprietor of a divine torture chamber, adept at knowing just when to lay off so that we won't lose heart and put an end to the test. It also places the minister in a position of moral ascendancy rather than a stance of compassionate service, since anyone who has collapsed under the weight of such measured burdens is implicitly a spiritual failure. One wonders how we have put our faith in a God who wields such control over life and yet uses it to toy with us so as to derive pleasure from our pain.

We have all encountered sincere believers who claim to have surrendered ultimate control of their lives to God in the certitude that the Lord is eager to take over the helm. God may well be our life's copilot, but we can certainly cite numerous crash landings despite such divine helmsmanship. While the Gospel of the storm at sea teaches a central faith truth, one wonders if its core has been missed in the past. Would a God who is Lord of the elements not drive the storm clouds away from the flooded Mississippi basin and over the drought stricken plains of Africa? If God can construct natural wonders, what are we to make of apparent divine passivity in the face of the world's "natural blunders?"

We may need to refashion our image of God as "cosmic air traffic controller" if the Lord's investment in our welfare is to continue to hold meaning for our faith lives.

Such a conversion might begin with our realization of a second divine quality: dynamism. The Lord is dynamic rather than static, setting power in motion instead of holding it at bay. In an age when power is sought to preserve the status quo in places like South Africa, we witness how much God's might is released toward transformation, conversion. Once power is set in motion, precise control over its direction and effect is forfeited. To control power statically is to limit its availability and force; to release power dynamically is to relinquish personal design over the details of its influence. Our God is not in control because she has preferred the multi-dimensional risks of dynamic power to the safe, controlled environment of static power. The Lord is a God of mystery, adventure, and surprise rather than explanation, safety, and boredom.

3. God Makes "Mistakes"/Has "Accidents"

I love the scene from the film *Oh God!* where George Burns, as God, casually admits to one of his disciples that "tobacco was one of my big mistakes." He goes on to include ostriches ("silly looking things") and avocados ("I made the pit too big"). He follows all this up by remarking: "You try!" Well, at least from the standpoint of human experience, "God" is absolutely right: creation and life itself are not perfect. We must develop and live out our faith in the context of a flawed environment.

Now this is a difficult concept to run with because it rubs against the grain of our piety and reverence. So, some things need to be kept in mind while considering this point. First, it is a pastoral rather than a theological category, employed for its role in setting up the ministerial perspective assumed later in the book. Secondly, the word "mistake" is used here as a human symbol rather than a cosmic literalism, a denial of the glory of the universe. It aims to realize that initial and very human prayer response to life's tragedy and ambiguity: "There must be some mistake." This reaction is part of the denial stage of the death and dying process. Finally, one might bring a sense of humor to this reflection to fully grasp its intended spirit.

Still, we cannot shy away from the truth that experience teaches us, especially while we continue to base our pastoral practice on the reliability of natural law. The natural law theory is built on the belief that God's system can be trusted to make the world work "naturally" without human interference. In this context we can only respond to life's inexplicable tragedies, knowing that they have not turned out well naturally (for example, a baby born into a family of starving Africans), by calling them "mistakes." Anything else leads us to conclude that God is a monster who has built terrible booby traps into nature. In fact, moral theologies that allow for the human intervention of artificial birth control are based on a judgment that in the unfolding of natural law, God's plan, there are "errors" which require "correction." More on this later.

Another way of expressing this, which may be more palatable to our faith's sensibilities, is to refer to life's unexplainable misfortunes as "divine accidents." This way of thinking is actually a vindication for a God who was often regarded as doing cruel things to us deliberately or willfully. If it sounds irreverent to refer to misfortunes as divine mistakes, is it any less impious to call them God's will? It seems much more consistent with reality and with our regard for God's goodness to say that many evils occur not by God's will (on purpose), but by accident (they are accidental to the working out of God's plan). This will be important when we take up an approach to ministry in the second half of the book.

4. God Is Not "My Personal God"

How nice it was to grow up in the fifties and have my own personal deity. This God carefully attended to every moment of my existence, knew what I was doing at all times (which led to some embarrassing moments in the bathroom), and took personal charge of the details of my life. Whatever reservations we had about the theological feasibility of this setup were alleviated by our faith in guardian angels. If our divine air traffic controller, monitoring billions of unpredictable blips, got distracted by a crisis on the screen, our guardian angels would fill the gap until the emergency was over. The symbolic truth of this scenario should not be lost upon us, but its literalistic overtones created theological and pastoral pitfalls.

In time it was our reflection upon personal tragedies, cruel ironies, and dumb luck which called this system into question and set us in search of sound theological alternatives. We came to understand that the realities of life call us to redefine our faith notion of a personal God. Such redefinition does not mean the death of faith without its rebirth, as illustrated by a simple encounter in the film *Gandhi*. In that scene Gandhi and a missionary are confronted on the street by racist youths. When the crisis passes without incident the priest sighs with relief: "That was lucky." Gandhi reacts at once: "I thought you were a man of God!" The priest's humorous reply belies its truth: "I am, but I'm not so egotistical as to think he plans his day around my dilemmas."

There are many pastoral implications to the notion of a personal God, especially as it was interpreted as I was growing up. These will be taken up later in the book. For now, it should be noted that Jesus very clearly taught us to pass over the notion of a personal God in the sense that we would regard the Lord as "my God." Instead, Jesus told us: "This, then, is how you should pray: 'Our Father in heaven'." God is not "my God," but rather "Our God." God is still personal, but in a much different sense, as we will see when we discuss ministry in particular.

God as Computer Programmer

It is the problem of evil, posed by stories of limit and loss, which reshapes the rosy image of God given us in youth. What image of God can we fashion which speaks the divine power and love we experience without contradicting the limits and pain we also encounter? Is God the personal Lord of Jewish tradition, the uninvolved God of Deism, the wrathful God of fundamentalism, the "pie in the sky" of existentialism, or the Incarnate Savior of Christianity? Do any of these images coincide with all of our encounters with God? If not, can we form such an image or images which will allow our faith to process questions which may seem like insurmountable obstacles? I would like to suggest one possible image which, while imperfect, may help us name our rich and mystifying experience of the Divine Being.

An image which has helped me sort out my experience in a satisfying way is that of God as the ultimate computer programmer. Life is the program which the Lord has written and the world is the computer it runs on. This image allows for our experience of the splendor and power of God (any program reflects the genius and creative power of its author), while also being consistent with life's misfortune and ambiguity (all programs have variables which randomly affect other factors even while facilitating their ultimate purpose). In moving through this reflection I caution the reader to hold in check common notions of computers as impersonal entities.

The weakness of this image is the danger that God, people, or the universe be regarded as machine-like or automated in the Newtonian sense. While a computer is a machine, a program is a living product of imagination, full of variables and possibilities, as well as risks, for those who will interact with or participate in it.

God, then, has created a marvelous system and a program designed to achieve an ultimate purpose: the coming of the kingdom. That program is invested with the life and power of its creator, a fact that is reinforced by the Lord's willingness to become part of the program. The Disney film *Tron* is an ingenious parable of a programmer who enters the world of his own program in order to redeem its ultimate purpose. Yet, once the Lord's "software" is running, its variables interact with each other and may produce chaotic and unintended results even while retaining their potential to achieve an ultimate design. The introduction of personal freedom into the program, for example, creates havoc as well as glory; the variable of rain allows for floods along with the irrigation of crops.

I love watching my sons play computer games. When things go wrong it is a revelation to witness them begin to grapple with the computer, which has become a very personal force to them in the unfolding of the game. They complain about any glitch which costs them points, or a "life," or ultimate victory. They struggle to accept my explanation that the computer is simply running a program and that if they are to play they must accept its "bugs" along with its wonders.

All of us are children of God, engaged in his marvelous computer game called life. If we are to play this game we must be ready for its glories and its tragedies, conscious of the fact that the program has ultimate aims which may not always be consistent with our immediate designs. We are right to complain to the master programmer for his part in our defeats in the best tradition of the psalms. Yet, we must also recall that God is respecting the ultimate integrity and purpose of the program and in so doing has sacrificed some of the control we might like to see exercised in order to suit our comfort. So, while we do not "let God off the hook" for life's dark side, neither should we become atheists because of the ambiguities of human existence.

I would invite the reader to play with this model of the world in whatever way is helpful. For now it is only necessary to see how this image of God and the world allows for both the glories and the mistakes of life and of God. It includes the glory of God insofar as "the Spirit" of the programmer is ever present as the program runs. It allows for divine "accidents" in that once the program is running the programmer cannot alter the chaotic influences of its variables upon one another without undermining their integrity and jeopardizing the ultimate goal of the system. All in all, as George Burns declares in *Oh God!*, the world can work: "I made it so it can work."

Hero Worship and Parental Almightiness

In the end, we all desperately need heroes to fight the battles of life for us (symbolically) or with us (actually). The forming and altering of our image of God is in reality the process of choosing a hero and giving him or her the qualities which we deem necessary to emerge victorious from life's struggles. Our hero, the Lord, is a precarious mixture of those traits which our fantasies judge vital to victory and those which are actually helpful. Each new experience changes that balance as we view the battle more clearly and comprehend how victory may best be won.

The contest on Mt. Carmel between Elijah and the prophets of Baal is an exquisite mythic story of a God-hero image in action. Most of us grew up with a picture of our parents as conquering heroes: "My dad can beat your dad"; "My Mom is prettier than your mom." In the same vein, Elijah reveals an early Hebrew image of our God-hero: "Our God can show up your god." Later this view of God would be challenged by a Messiah who met all such illusions with a proclamation of the centrality of the cross: "The Son of Man must suffer much and be rejected by the elders" (Mark 8/31).

In our youth we drew great comfort from our image of our parents as conquering heroes. We felt safe in the knowledge that they could provide us with every good thing and protect us from all harm. As our family life proceeded, however, we were confronted with experiences which called upon us to redefine our images of our parents and of heroism itself. The very qualities we once valued as heroic gradually proved to make our parents distant and unapproachable: "I could never live up to my dad's expectations" or "I could never be the person my mother is." Similarly, the very qualities we once viewed as signs of weakness (vulnerability and limits) became associated with true heroism in that they allowed us to identify and communicate with our parents.

My father died when I was a junior in high school. I recall the time surrounding the funeral and the funeral rite itself as a kind of summary of the image my family had of him while he was alive. While it was never explicitly expressed as such, I came away with a picture of my father as a man of faith who nobly and peacefully accepted his death by cancer, ready and eager to be united with his God in heaven. It was only years later that my mom told me that dad was quite "unprepared" to die. He wanted to live longer and spend more time with the family he loved (he had "lost" three of his sons to the seminary at age 13). He simply desired to experience more of the life he cherished.

This portrait of a man who was quite vulnerable and human was a stark contrast to my "faith" in him as a saint, a rock to the end who was quite unattached to this mundane existence. I thank my mother for supplying this revelation of my father which allowed me to change my image of the god of my childhood and worship him in a new way, a way much more helpful to me in my own journey. So it is that as our myths about our parents are challenged we have the choice of clutching the ideal by altering the evidence, or letting go and allowing the old

idol to be reshaped into a new image, more worthy of
our worship and more life-giving in the kind of power it
offers.

Our journey of faith, as the fashioning of a workable
and lifegiving God-hero image, works in the same way.
Will our God be invincible and perfect, and therefore
unapproachable and inimitable, or will God be
vulnerable and "imperfect," and thus intimate and
incarnate? There are plenty of reasons to opt for
warrior gods (Rambo, Dirty Harry, Robocop) amid the
fragility of modern life. Yet, to close this chapter I
would suggest the God-parent image painted by the film
Ordinary People.

In the closing moments of that film there is a
Father-Son (God-child) encounter which is a
microcosm of the journey we are invited to take in the
development of our God-hero image. The father, just
separated from his wife, is joined in the yard by his
teenage son who is recovering from a recent suicide
attempt. Throughout the film the father has struggled to
minister to his son's pain even as the personal issues
that hurt raised were making him increasingly
vulnerable. So it is that his son thanks him for the gift he
had to always make the family feel safe while he was
growing up, like things would work out. "I always
admired you for that," he says. The father, newly aware
of his limits, remarks: "Don't admire people too much;
they'll disappoint you sometimes." Then the teen's
transformed image of his father gives rise to his reply:
"I'm not disappointed; I love you!"

It seems to me this is exactly the journey to mature faith that each of us travels. We experience our Divine Parent as almighty in our youth and we appropriately worship God for the security that faith provides. At this point we may hear God's subtle warning: "Don't admire me too much, I'll disappoint you sometimes." Then, sure enough, as the realities of life press upon us, we witness how much God shares our vulnerability and weakness, especially in Jesus. Faced with this "disappointment" we may choose to deny our experience and cling to our fading "almighty God-hero." We may flee to even more unrealistic but comforting gods like Rambo. Finally, our journey brings us to that point where we yield to a new, more life-giving God-hero: "I'm not disappointed; I love you!" How we respond to this challenge of reshaping our God-hero image according to the mold of the Paschal Mystery will have great implications for our pastoral life, as we will see in the coming chapters.

Items for Individual Reflection/Group Process

1. What does it mean to you as you recite the Creed each week to profess your faith in "God the Father Almighty?" Has life changed your definition of divine power? How?

2. Recall an experience when God "let you down." How did you reconcile that event with your image of God's omnipotence at the time?

3. Do you have the feeling that God is in control of your life? What exactly does that mean? What evidence supports your faith? Did you have a different sense of how God managed your life as a youth? How and in what way did it change?

4. The author employs the words "mistake" and "accident" to describe the human experience of the breakdown of divine power. Does this make sense to you? Does it seem irreverent? In view of the point the writer is making, is there another word you would prefer to describe that experience? Explain.

5. Is the notion of God as a "personal God" vital to your faith? How do you react to the author's claim that God should not be regarded as "my personal God" in the manner we were taught as children? How do you explain the logistical problems created by such a notion (e.g., God the air traffic controller allowing "mid-air collisions")?

6. How did the concept of "personal God" contribute to the rise of privatized religion? Did it affect you in that way? How?

7. Relate your journey of faith with God to your parental relationships. Have you struggled to accept your "real parents" as opposed to your ideal image of them? Has this struggle been mirrored in your faith relationship with God, your divine Mother

and Father? Has your acceptance and love of limited human parents expedited your coming to terms with a limited divine parent? In what way?

8. Does the image of God as a divine computer programmer work for you? What are its strengths and weaknesses? Is it too impersonal? Does it express the unyieldingness ("bugs") of life as you experience it? What other images help reflect such hard realities about God and life?

9. The author describes God, instead of being "almighty," as One who "gives power away" and "sets power in motion." Consider these points in relationship to the ways power is sought and used in contemporary society. What lessons might we learn from a God who refuses to seek almightiness in the ways we do?

Activities for Pastoral Staffs/Ministries

1. Draw a "flow chart" of how power is operative in your parish or staff. What does that diagram say about the perceived balance of divine and human work in ministry? Draw an ideal flow chart representing this "balance of power" and note how the two compare. What ramifications does this comparison hold for ministry?

2. Write a letter to your parents, whether living or dead (this letter is for your benefit, not theirs). Relate your delights and letdowns in growing up with them. Then write a similar letter to God. Compare the two and note their implications for your development as a pastoral person or team.

3. View the last five minutes of *It's a Wonderful Life* and *Ordinary People*. Compare their endings and your reactions to them with a view toward understanding your ministry as an individual; as a team.

4. Discuss the Church's teaching of Papal Infallibility. Does this doctrine speak of an ecclesial desire to tap into God's power as a "mistake-proof" minister? What are the benefits and liabilities of such an identification and why is it being challenged today? Is this doctrine related to modern cultural heroes who personify our desire for invulnerability? Does your ministry seek to be identified as "infallible," or is there an admission of "fall-ability"?

5. Make a list of your personal heroes as a child, whether real or fictional. Next, list those whom you regard as heroes at this point in your life. Contrast the two lists. How do the qualities of the two groups compare? What changes in you do their differences point out?

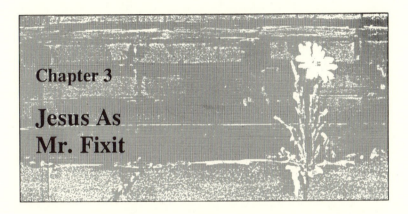

Chapter 3

Jesus As
Mr. Fixit

"Clean up your room or there'll be no supper for you!"
— Parent to child

Is there any experience in Catholic life more
associated with innocence and perfection than a child's
First Communion? True to the symbolism of the white
dresses and shirts worn by the children, the day of First
Communion overflows with a sense of blessedness
(purity, goodness, order) and divine presence (God is
here). Such feelings are true and proper to sacramental
events and are to be fostered in their celebration. Yet,
all liturgical moments occur in the larger context of life
and retain their authenticity to the extent that they
articulate and give birth to the faith with which
experience is pregnant.

Sacraments are "islands in the stream" in the way that they afford us opportunities to gain a perspective on the river of life for the purpose of re-entering the flow with greater purpose and energy. In order to appreciate the graceful moment of First Communion, then, it is appropriate as well to study the life context within which that "island" is situated. This is especially important in view of the fact that liturgy symbolizes life for us (more will be said about this later). If rites are celebrated out of context as moments of purity and order, it may well be natural to generalize that experience to a viewpoint of life as perfect or orderly. The result is the possibility that the life of perfection will be canonized as the only way to "make God present."

As a professional religious educator I have been involved in the preparation, planning, and celebration of many Communion ceremonies. It was only recently, however, that I knew my first experience with First Eucharist as a father. My stepson, Mark, celebrated First Communion a few years ago, and I anticipated it to be much like so many of the rites I had witnessed from a professional perspective. The life context of our "blended family," however, introduced some interesting variables which were to dramatically undermine that expectation.

A few days prior to First Communion day there arose a dispute over the manner in which custody of the children would be divided between the parents for that weekend. This conflict was complicated by the fact that the matter was not specifically covered in the divorce agreement. By the day before the ceremony the problem had still not been resolved. So it was that preparations for this event unfolded in quite an untidy fashion.

At mid-afternoon the phone rang. It was our lawyer, who was continuing to negotiate the issues raised a few days earlier. A conference call was arranged and a settlement was reached calling for an equal division of custody for the weekend. Things did not prove to be quite that easy, however, as the dispute flared up again that evening. There were threats of court orders, contacts with local police, and some angry personal confrontations both on the phone and at our front door. Tension was thick in the air and the kids were crying by evening's end. Eric, our other son, sadly summarized the experience by remarking: "This is the kind of thing that would make me avoid marriage altogether."

So, there we were the next day, sitting in the same pew with Mark, waiting for the celebration to begin. Yet, in view of all that had happened, how could we celebrate and what would we be celebrating? I recall looking around and thinking of all the times I had stood before groups just like this and spoken of the joy and beauty of the day, the loving presence of Jesus that we would experience. I wondered how many people had heard me say those words and thought: "If he only knew...," or "Who is he kidding?!" Now it was my turn, our turn, to face the challenge of naming the presence of Jesus among us, among the very people who had been entangled in a bitter dispute the night before. It was our task to "save the day" for Mark, to minister to him in a way that would redeem the presence of Jesus and rescue the symbolic truth of his white shirt in the midst of the messy realities of divorce lawyers, police, and court orders.

The Conditions of Divine Presence

The purpose of this chapter is to look at the meaning of Jesus's coming in the context of the two ministerial perspectives suggested by the story above. The first perspective, symbolized by the professional minister, the "outsider," views the pure and serene world of First Communion as a sign of Jesus's unmitigated presence wherever such innocence and perfection exist. The second perspective, personified by the person in the pew, looks with terror at the mess that abounds in his/her life and wonders whether Jesus is anywhere to be found or how he might be made to be present in such an unlikely place ("Lord I am not worthy...").

The question of Jesus's presence in any particular place or circumstance, then, is an inquiry into the conditions for his coming. That question is central for the minister, whether professional or amateur. In each period of church history ministry has been shaped by definite notions of the necessary conditions for Christ's gracious presence. Those presuppositions reveal a great deal about our conception of the mission of Jesus, and indeed, our image of the Divine Parent who sent him. The present generation of adult Christians grew up with the assumptions of the pre-Vatican II church and the

image of God upon which its ministry was based.
Accordingly, when Christians raised in that milieu
attempt to get inside God's head to trace the process by
which the mission of Jesus unfolded in the divine
imagination, a scenario something like what follows
might be painted:

It is the seventh day and God is gazing blissfully down
upon creation, weary (six "God-days" is a mighty long
work week) but satisfied that all the hard work has paid
off. The Creator is noting how particularly well Adam
and Eve are preserving the perfection and order of the
divine handiwork. Suddenly Eve is spotted heading for
the tree of forbidden fruit. Apprehensive, God steps
outside the pearly gates for a closer look. From this
ideal vantage point the Creator watches as Eve bites the
apple, shares it with Adam, and everything begins to go
to pot. "Oh no! My perfect creation is ruined! How
could I have trusted those two with such a work of art?
If they think I'm going to stick around and watch as they
ruin my pride and joy they have another thing coming!"
With that God storms back into heaven and slams the
gates shut to close out sinful humankind, much as a
parent who has walked in on a child with a messy room
closes the door saying: "You're not coming out until
this mess is cleaned up!"

Although a caricature, this passage reflects one
authentic image of the Divine Parent as someone who
abhors a mess. God would not be caught dead in a mess
and isn't very excited about the prospect of hanging
around those who make messes. Our Lord much prefers
neatness, spotless perfection, and order. Accordingly, to

be neat and clean and to pick up after ourselves are high priority items for our Creator. The mission of Jesus stems directly from these values lodged in the "heart of hearts" of our heavenly Parent. With this in mind we are ready to continue our caricature to discover how the mission of Jesus, as we were taught to imagine it, might have first been conceived.

The Creator has been stewing over things down on earth for quite a while now. God has been watching recent developments, hoping for a reversal of the trend, but is honest enough to admit that little improvement has been made. Even divine efforts to help out once in a while have proved fruitless ("Moses even broke my Ten Commandments, of all things"). Finally, depressed and frustrated, God decides that enough is enough! It's time to send in the cavalry:

Creator: "Jesus, get down there and clean that up!"

Jesus: "Oh come on; I didn't do it!"

Creator: "I don't care. I want you to restore order."

Jesus: "Couldn't you just send another flood?"

Creator: "That's just a temporary measure. Besides, it was kind of messy too in its own way."

Jesus: "What do I have to do?"

Creator: "I want you to become one of them, a carpenter; that way you might be able to fix things up."

Jesus: "Oh, alright, but I'm not going down there for long! After the job's done I'll form a maintenance crew to keep things in order so I can take off."

Creator: "Don't forget your overalls."

Jesus: "Very funny."

This image of Jesus as the ultimate maintenance man, fixing a "broken world," cleaning up after our mess, and establishing a workforce to "sweep up" while he's gone, rings fairly true as the picture I was given while growing up Catholic. I believe it still represents a fairly common Christian understanding of the Divine Parent's reason for sending the Son as Redeemer.

Jesus, then, becomes the ultimate symbol of the Creator's overriding passion for neatness and our constant tendency toward messiness. It is a cosmic replay of *The Odd Couple*. God is Felix, never quite able to dwell with us or to relax in our presence without chiding us for our sloppiness and straightening up a bit. We, of course, are Oscar, basically sincere and good-natured, but with that irritating penchant for making a mess which makes us most difficult to live with. Jesus acts as maid-servant to enable all to dwell at peace in the Divine Parent's house. The Lord mediates the divine-human feud by initiating and overseeing the cleanup. Without Jesus the Creator will never come to our room (the world) and open the door (the gates of heaven) so that we may once again come out (into the Kingdom) and be part of the family (children of God).

Will the Real Savior Please Stand Up?

While we grew up with this vision of the meaning of Jesus, and while it operated well enough for a time, one must wonder how it escaped us for so long how very inconsistent such a vision is with the life and ministry of

Jesus. A study of the values of Jesus, his teachings and interactions with people, and the very circumstances of his life, reveal a Savior quite removed from the neatness and perfection long associated with his mission.

Our Messiah plunged headlong into the messiness of human existence by taking on human flesh. He was born into a life of poverty amidst earth, straw, and animals. Raised a carpenter, he did hard work and lived among common people. He prepared for his mission by going into the wilds, the wilderness of the desert. In his public ministry he constantly shunned the convenience of regular food and lodging: "...the Son of Man has no where to lay his head." His bloody death was itself the result of his refusal to "play the Messiah" by being the neat, conquering warrior that many expected. The following comparison between Jesus and Rambo as saviors reveals the radical nature of our choice of Messiahs:

Rambo as Savior

- saves by killing for us.
- followers witness him killing their captors.
- "new life" and freedom come out of the death of others.
- actions teach the hatred and destruction of enemies.
- invites us to take up our weapons.

- victory through winning: "Do we get to win this time?"

- abandoned by those who sent him, he vows retaliation.

Jesus as Savior

- saves by dying for us.

- followers witness him dying at the hands of captors.

- new life and freedom born out of his own death.

- actions teach the love and forgiveness of enemies.

- invites us to "put away our swords."

- victory through defeat: "The Son of Man must suffer!"

- abandoned by the One who sent him, he surrenders his spirit.

The words of Jesus during his public life constantly upset and puzzled people rather than neatly resolving their dilemmas. Are we to describe as logical a teaching ministry which holds that to be first we must be last, to keep we must let go, and to live we must die? The fact that paradox was a hallmark of Jesus's teaching reflects his refusal to become an "answer man." When challenged in the play *Godspell* regarding his dodging of questions, Jesus replies: "Did I ever promise you an answer to the question?" The parable of the wheat and weeds (Matt 13/24-30) is Christ's proclamation of a Father who is comfortable with the messiness of life, not one who is eager to "weed out the garden."

The most telling sign of Jesus's ministerial style, however, is his constant preference for spending time with the sinner and the outcast (the messy). Nothing was more confusing and annoying to the Lord's critics, not to mention his followers, than this. He actually went so far as to make sinfulness (messiness) a pre-requisite to his presence: "People who are well do not need a doctor, but only those who are sick"; "Tax collectors and sinners will enter the kingdom before you."

Jesus continually surprised people by his disregard for their engrained conviction that God shies away from sinners: "Zacchaeus, come down, for I must stay in your house today." The woman at the well believed that ministry was only possible when her life was under control: "I don't have a husband." The Lord showed her that true ministry could only begin once it was understood that her life was messy: "You have had five husbands, and the man you are living with now is not your husband." For Jesus, the vision of the man born blind surpassed the self-proclaimed sight of the Pharisees. How significant it is that Jesus cured this man's blindness by smearing his eyes with mud.

Jesus Elects the Poor as Housekeepers

Jesus boldly proclaimed that it is the poor who have
first claim on the Kingdom: "Blessed are the poor;
theirs is the Kingdom of Heaven." The rich have first
claim on neat and orderly lives. With their money the
rich can buy the "neatness" of an abortion, the calm of a
valium, the protection of a lawyer, the favor of a
politician, the way out of a dilemma. It is only the rich
who can afford to hire professional maids, servants, and
gardeners to handle the housework and make life
convenient. The guests of the wealthy learn to expect a
spotless household when they arrive, for they know that
the tidying up has been done by the hired help, who
then go off to their own separate living quarters which
they must maintain. Moreover, any blemish puts a
damper on the guest's stay, for among the rich one
learns to be put off by imperfection.

The poor, on the other hand, are those most at the
mercy of life's messiness. When the hard realities of life
come crashing down upon them, they cannot afford to
buy their way out. The destitute must maintain their
own dwellings, often after attending to the
establishments of their rich employers. At times they
are simply too tired to do all they would like toward the
upkeep of their homes. Their friends, well acquainted
with such realities, come to expect the discomfort and
imperfection that attend the lot of the poor. The guests
of the lowly learn to appreciate the other gifts that

compensate for what is lacking. The life and ministry of Jesus proclaims that it is these poor with whom God is pleased and comfortable to dwell.

The Lord's preference for the company of the poor and his invitation that we all become poor calls us back to our earlier reflection upon the birth of the Savior's mission in the imagination of our Divine Parent. In light of our brief overview of the hallmarks of Christ's ministry a rather different scenario is likely. As we revisit the Creator's heavenly dwelling, we find God again surveying the unfolding of life below. Our heavenly Parent is again depressed, but this time for a different reason. The conversation which ensues reveals a "different God" and provides a clue to the key of ministry in a messy world.

Creator: "Jesus, we've got to do something!"

Jesus: "What's wrong?"

Creator: "Things are so messy down there that I'm afraid people are beginning to conclude that I'm not with them."

Jesus: "Well, the story of the Flood did make a big splash!"

Creator: "Cute! But, that's just the problem; they're starting to misconstrue the world itself as a sign of my absence and displeasure."

Jesus: "Well, in all fairness, the world is the only sign they have."

Creator: "Then they need a new sign!"

Jesus: "How about if I become one of them, living proof of where your heart really lies?"

Creator: "A marvelous idea! It would show them that I am closer than they ever imagined, part of even the messiest aspects of their lives."

Jesus: "I'll get right on it!"

Who, then, is Jesus for us and how can we make his presence a reality in the world? To answer this question I would like to return to the First Communion ceremony with which I began this reflection and to the two ministerial perspectives that story suggested.

It seems to me that we cannot identify the meaning of Jesus, as I often did, with the person of the religious educator looking out over the serene, pure world of a First Communion ceremony. This sort of professional "naivete" presumes an image of a Lord who in present and active mainly in those "perfect moments" of our lives, even as it misses the illusory quality of such unmitigated bliss. Nor can we associate the ministry of Jesus with that moment of panic we felt as parents after the turbulent events of the night before. Such a sense that "all is lost" is a sign of our faith in a Messiah who is remote to such untidy circumstances and a subtle rejection of our own participation in the mission of Jesus.

If we wait for those moments associated with the presence of Jesus to be perfect, then we miss the point of his "imperfect coming" and forfeit the ability to experience the constancy and intimacy of his presence here. Jesus is the model "minister in a messy world" and we are called to follow in his muddy footsteps. We must let go of our image of Jesus as cosmic maintenance man, ultimate incarnation of a Creator who patrols the dwellings of our world with white gloves on, running a finger over the surfaces of our lives to see if we pass the neatness test. Indeed, church policies which require primary children to confess their sins before receiving the Eucharist get a regrettable head start at hammering home this notion of God (more will be said about this later). Jesus is the living reminder of a Parent who jumps down in the thick of things, rolls up those divine sleeves, and calls out: "Here I am; let's get to work!" Our ministry can be nothing less if it is to mirror such a God-Parent.

So it was that the mess did not go away that day at Mark's First Communion. There was tension in the pew. Eric, who was sitting between myself and his father said afterwards: "I've never been so glad to see a Mass end!" Yet, God was present. Indeed, only as the crisis at hand called upon us to "be the body of Christ" for Mark and for the family was the presence of Jesus revealed which allowed Mark to "receive communion." Thus, Mark moved back and forth between the family groups as mediator and sign of peace, a reincarnation of the Lord's body. We even took pictures for each other after Mass. So, in a limited but real way we shared a common bond that transcended the "bonds" of division and anger, a sign of a possible future: the Kingdom. In other words, the mess did not go away, but neither did the Lord. It seems to me that this is what Eucharist is all about: becoming bread broken so that all might be made one in the sharing. That may also be a fairly precise meaning for the coming of Jesus.

Items for Individual Reflection/Group Process

1. Who was Jesus for you as a child (who was that "masked man")?
   Who is he for you today? How has Jesus's identity changed for
   you over the years? What brought about these changes?

2. What was your perception of the mission of Jesus as a youth?
   What would you identify as the primary mission of Jesus today?
   Reflect upon the meaning of any changes that have occurred.

3. Do you agree with the author that Jesus was pictured as a sort of
   "clean up man" after the mess made by original sin? Why or why
   not? Discuss the suggestion that Jesus came into the world, not as
   Redeemer, but as Reminder. What was he here to remind us of?
   How does this change the purpose of ministry?

4. Recall your impressions of your First Communion day. What did
   that event communicate about Jesus? about you? Now remember
   your first confession, which probably preceded the Eucharist.
   What did the position and experience of that rite of Penance
   express about Jesus?; about you?; about sacramental ministry?

5. If you have or had children today, would you want them to make
   first Reconciliation prior to celebrating First Communion? Why
   or why not? Do you feel a gut instinct to make Reconciliation a
   way of "cleaning up your act" for the coming of Jesus (e.g.,
   sacraments, Christmas, Easter)? How might we develop a more
   positive style of preparation for the Lord's coming?

6. How do you think we "forgot" the Lord's preference for hanging
   around with sinners and outcasts (Zacchaeus, Woman at the well,
   Man born blind)? How might we continue the process of re-
   membering the church through that preference?

7. Remember a time when you felt particularly unworthy to have the
   Lord "come under your roof." Who "spoke but the Word" that
   made your soul healed? Might the healing that allows Jesus to

come be an interior conversion which realizes our
"unworthiness" as an impediment of limited human imagination
rather than as a divine restriction?

8. Discuss the many ways that Jesus refused to be an answer man.
Why did he speak in such obtuse, convoluted ways? Was there a
method to this madness? What was it?

9. In *The Last Temptation of Christ*, what was the temptation? Was
this temptation different in the eyes of the director than it was in
the view of the film's critics? Is humanity God's temptation? Is
marriage a temptation or a sacrament? What is the real sin that
Jesus is tempted by in this film?

Activities for Pastoral Staffs/Ministries

1. Study various images of Jesus as portrayed in films, artworks, crucifixes, songs, etc. (e.g., Jesus as shown in *Jesus Christ Superstar, Jesus of Nazareth, Godspell,* and *The Last Temptation of Christ*). Discuss the differences, both blatant and subtle, in these images as well as why you accept or reject them. What image of Christ does the artwork in your parish or community promote? Is it time for a change?

2. Gather those responsible for First Communion preparation in your parish or community. What level of sensitivity exists in the group regarding the messy circumstances many people bring to this ideal celebration (unchurched, divorced, mixed faith, single parent)? What can be done to improve this sensitivity and give it concrete expression.?

3. Read the biblical passage regarding the purpose of parables (Luke 8/9-10). What does this reference say regarding our purpose as ministers? Consider the leanings of the group, for example, toward the contrasting poles of either literalism or symbolism, of either asking questions or providing answers in ministry.

4. Parish leaders might assess their commitment to developing adult education as part of their readiness to enter an age of ministry in a messy world. A good start is an appraisal of to what extent child-centered programs have promoted a "cutesy" notion of faith and sacrament in the parish. This commonly occurs when events like First Communion and Christmas pageants become the focus of adult (parental) faith through their kids ("Isn't that cute!"). This is not a problem except in the frequency with which such faith distracts the adult and forms an obstacle to facing the real core of Christianity, which is very grownup and gritty at its center. The staff might ask these questions with a view toward keeping "cute faith" in its place and engaging adult Christians in the pressing issues of the day.

5. Browse a video rental store. Note the number of films that
   degrade humanity, especially women. Discuss why films that
   depict God in human terms cause such an uproar while movies
   that portray people in less than human terms are popular. To
   what extent does our ministry hinge upon popular notions of the
   divine and the human?

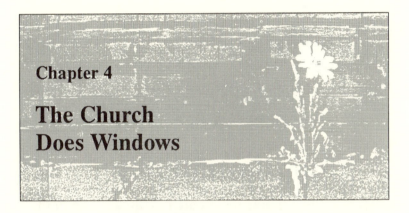

Chapter 4

The Church Does Windows

"It would have been alright if there hadn't been any mess; but you can't handle mess. You need everything neat and easy."
— from the film *Ordinary People*

Throughout the film *Ordinary People*, Conrad Jarrett fights to recover from his suicide attempt. Much of that struggle is played out against the backdrop of his relationship with his parents, particularly his mother. Conrad's inability to accept himself and his life is mirrored and intensified by his mother's failure to cope with the reality of their situation. Beth is constantly at odds with her son over what sometimes appear to be trivial matters. Yet, these conflicts carry a very definite message for Conrad, a message of non-forgiveness and alienation.

This issue surfaces in one of Conrad's sessions with his psychiatrist. He claims that he will never be forgiven for all that he has done. When the psychiatrist, in searching for one example of such transgressions, attempts to write off the suicide attempt as "water under the bridge," Conrad responds vehemently: "I'm never going to be forgiven for that; never! You can't get it out, all the blood on her towels and her rug. Everything had to be pitched! She fired the goddamned maid because she couldn't dust the living room right."

Church Maintenance and Ministry

Here is the ultimate nightmare of a breakdown of the ministerial bond between parent and child over an inability to accept the messiness of that commitment. This story, in view of the fact that the church symbolizes the pastoral connection between God-parent and God-children, poses a similar challenge for us. If, as I have suggested, we follow in the ministerial footsteps of a Savior whom we have often regarded as a divine fix-it man, then that challenge assumes new proportions. When the reconciliation accomplished by Jesus is interpreted as reparation (repair-ation) we become increasingly prone to identify ourselves as a divine maintenance crew left behind by the Lord to make sure his efforts are not laid waste by messy human existence.

Once this image of ecclesial custodian is planted in our pastoral sensibilities, the commission of the church by Jesus assumes its logic. Accordingly, the call to "Go, then, to all peoples everywhere and make them my disciples, baptizing them in the name of the Father, the Son, and the Holy Spirit" can easily be heard as a mandate to construct a huge spiritual bath-house which produces disciples by cleaning them up. The statement: "Whose sins you shall forgive, they are forgiven..." can be taken as a bestowal of the power to conduct hearings to determine whose houses merit the seal of approval and whose are to be condemned. The suggestion that we "shake the dust from our feet" might be regarded as a license to limit our involvement with those whose lives are "beyond repair."

Yet, few could accuse the modern church of being dominated by such a pastoral image. Even our staunchest critics would be hard pressed to argue that the church has distanced herself from the messiest realities of contemporary life. So, while the custodial image continues to influence the pastoral prerogatives of the church, perhaps that influence is more subtle than blatant, holding more sway over the ranking of pastoral priorities than over the stipulation of exclusive choices. In that case the pastoral dilemma of a community swayed by the maintenance model of ministry might be accurately played out in a familiar scenario.

Consider the dedicated parent busily preparing dinner while engaging in the mental gymnastics required to juggle the hectic schedule of the coming work week. Nearby in the highchair sits Megan, happily but messily devouring a trayful of strained foods. Suddenly an unexplainable impulse strikes and the infant launches the tray onto the floor where, true to Murphy's law, it lands upside down. Megan bursts into tears and dad turns to survey the scene. In that brief moment before better judgement can assert itself, instinct takes over. The parent points an accusing finger at the crying child and blurts out: "bad girl!" He then bends down and begins wiping up the mess. Afterwards he takes Megan in his arms and soothes the child's distress.

Natural and understandable as the parent's reaction may seem, it reveals a definite set of priorities, the operation of a value system. The question posed by this story is simple and direct: "What is more important: the messes that people make or the people who make them?" In times of crisis, where will our first efforts be directed?; what will be our pastoral priority? If our past training has predisposed us to respond first to the mess and second to the messy, then we must retrain ourselves so that such false instincts do not dictate our responses to human pastoral needs. If our image of the church speaks more of a maintenance orientation than of a nurturing one, then perhaps that image needs to be reshaped into a a more creative form.

Maybe if we take time to explore some alternative ecclesial models along these lines we may be led to a deeper consciousness of our ministerial options and their consequences. In so doing it is important to recall that such models exist upon a continuum whose opposite poles create a tension that can be quite healthy. The "negative poles" of the contrasting models we will consider here are a natural response to that traditional ecclesial mandate which called us to be "in the world but not of the world." For our purposes this "mission statement" might be paraphrased to read "in a messy world but not of a messy world." In any case, it is not our purpose here to choose one pole over the other, but to suggest a healthy synthesis between extremes. Above all we seek to engage in the theological reflection which will allow us to adopt models of the church which conceive increasingly pastoral priorities consistent with the Gospel and human experience.

Church as Forest Preserve or Garden

Our perception of the Garden of Eden as a state of primordial perfection recaptured by Jesus lends itself to an image of the church as a sort of cosmic forest preserve. Within those friendly confines the original beauty and order of creation can be maintained and protected from the forces that would prevail against it. In this scenario church ministers become park rangers whose task it is to patrol the grounds and enforce the rules which allow the utopian world to continue its existence. There is an awareness of imperfection, but such messiness is at least confined to the outer limits of specified boundaries.

Contrast this to an image of the church as a garden where people may grow as plants which embody the life of the Lord or as wheat which is harvested as food for the Body of Christ. In this world it is not the mission of the pastoral minister to uproot the weeds that threaten healthy plants, true to the Gospel parable of the wheat and the weeds, but to labor for a bountiful harvest within the limits (earthiness) of the land. Thus, the minister has stewardship of the entire Garden and may not ignore the weeds with their influence upon the overall productivity of the land. Such a minister will get his/her hands dirty working the land, but will rejoice at the beauty of a rich harvest.

Church as Window or Fireplace

In a world where God is offended by disorder, reluctant to cast light into life's dark corners for fear of the dust that may have collected there, the church becomes God's window into the world. Hesitant to completely withdraw divine light from life, God makes the church an exclusive portal of heavenly radiance. Since this light is scarce, not available in the public domain, it is the task of the minister to keep the window clean at all costs. Those children who dirty the window must repent and wipe off their smudges. Those who block the light by standing at the window and gazing out at the larger world are required to move. In this scenario church ministers proudly announce their propensity for doing windows. In the process, unfortunately, they are blinded to the wisdom of our liturgical environment which proclaims that "stained glass" is much more effective than transparent glass for revealing the glory of the Lord.

In Steinbeck's novel, *The Winter of Our Discontent*, Ethan Hawley comes to a numbing conclusion on the brink of a suicidal despair: "It isn't true that there's a community of light, a bonfire of the world. Everyone carries his own, his lonely own." Yet, even from the blackness of that pit he is able to glimpse the saving truth that light can be passed on from one to another. Ethan is saved by the realization of his responsibility to pass that light on to his daughter "else another light might go out." Thus, an alternative calling for a "window church" is the invitation to ignite this community of light, to be a fireplace for the world to gather around. Such fireplace or campfire light is born of those willing to pitch camp together and, as Dick Westley illustrates in *Redemptive Intimacy*, prepared to break camp and move on when called. This light is impossible to block out since it comes from within the people, within the community. The light can only be "blocked in" or held in: "No one lights a lamp and puts it under a basket; instead he puts it on the lampstand where it gives light for everyone in the house" (Matt 5/15).

Church as Library or Playhouse

Another significant pastoral dilemma facing the church today lies in the tension between the images of library and playhouse. The library is the place where stories are collected, shelved, and made available to patrons. While librarians promote reading and sometimes engage in storytelling, the most essential work of the librarian might well be regarded as the categorizing or naming of stories. The promotion of reading would be fruitless if disorder made the books hard to obtain. The playhouse, moreover, is the forum where stories are acted out on the stage for the public. Here the actor and director do their most vital and effective work when they make a script come alive by enacting it out of a connectedness with their own involvement in life, their personal stories. In modern theatre there is evidence of an increasing tendency to involve the audience in the performance. Let us take a few moments to explore these two models of church and the ministerial roles they incorporate.

On first glance it might seem easy to opt for the image of ecclesial playhouse over the library church. Yet, upon further study this is not such an obvious choice. The function of naming (entitling) is a powerful and sacramental human activity. The truth of the phrase "it's all in a name" should not be lost upon us here. The sacraments, after all, are about naming people as "children of God," "forgiven," "wedded," etc., so that the graceful realities they have already begun to experience will be deepened and shared (so that they will feel "entitled" to know and respond to such grace). So much of our faith would be lost if we didn't have liturgical moments with which to name common human experience as theological. How much of our personal development rests upon an ability and willingness to name something inside of us (a feeling, a truth, a gift, a sin) so that we can move creatively onward?

Yet, the limitations of naming should not be lost upon us either. Naming can so easily become categorizing and categorizing is not far removed from stereotyping. After all, it is the duty of a librarian to catalogue the story so that it can be easily identified and found. The librarian asks "What kind of story is this?" and comes up with a name and a place for that story. Is it fiction or fantasy or science or philosophy or history? Such questions have their practical advantages, but also carry the baggage of liabilities.

When something is named there is a gain, but there is also a loss. As soon as I call someone a saint I am more aware of their goodness, but do I also lose touch with their sanctifying limits and human approachability in the process? When I name someone a sinner I see their need, but do I implicitly place myself in an exalted position or cut them off from the communion of saints? When I identify a person as a man I immediately avail myself of certain masculine qualities, but do I risk disguising the wonders of the female side of him?

So it is that when we invoke the names "rich," "American," "liberal," "Catholic," "democrat," "handicapped," etc., truth is gained but truth is also lost. When I call a name I summon something true but I also cast a shadow over something just as real, albeit hidden or undeveloped. This may be why Yahweh was reluctant to reveal his name at the Israelites' bidding. God's people see the power of names, but are they fully aware of their limits and dangers? Jesus was also skeptical of names and cautioned those who used them too lightly: "Why do you call me good? No one is good except God alone" (Luke 18/19).

The ministerial response of the church in particular pastoral situations is based upon the name given the person or need at hand (e.g., inquirer, widow, sinner). While this is a helpful starting point, problems arise when ministry is limited by one's "given name," or worse, when the person or crisis doesn't fit any of our existing categories. The librarian has the option of creating a new category for a unique story, but with few entries for that category it is liable to get lost or ignored. Actors, however, have greater power to bring obscure stories before the public for the truth they hold or the artistic awareness they offer. The question before a naming/librarian and storytelling/playhouse church is this: How can these two self images be most effectively balanced toward refining the shape of our ministry?

The Limits of Naming Evoke the Power of Storytelling

Limbo is a symbol of a passing propensity for relying too heavily on the librarian model of church to define our ministry. The demise of the term "Limbo" from our ecclesial consciousness is also a sign of the limitations of that model. For a long time we knew that baptized people were saints and that the unbaptized were sinners and that each group would be sent to heaven or hell accordingly. Then a case came along that didn't fit into our existing categories, a case that we couldn't name: unbaptized but innocent babies. So, we invented a new category that was actually a non-category: Limbo. In

Limbo people neither quite see God nor quite lose God. Our incapacity to name those infants as children of God resulted in a corresponding disruption of ministry to their grieving parents. In our dilemma we told them: "Your child is with God, sort of," or "Your child isn't with God, but is completely happy otherwise."

While the concept of Limbo has drifted off into a limbo of its own, more subtle versions of the same dilemma continue to plague us. There are still categories of people who fall between the cracks of our current librarian catalogue system and ministry to them continues to be limited or neglected. We either don't know what we are legitimately commissioned to do for such groups because of their identities (we don't know where to put them on our shelves), or we don't know if we can number them among us because of the nature of their stories (we are not sure if they belong on our shelves at all). Examples of such groups are: the divorced and remarried, homosexuals, dissenting theologians, and women ministers.

Yet, the naming process need not forestall pastoral efforts. When the naming church is inadequate and people are "left in Limbo," we can employ the storytelling church in a complementary cycle until a "proper name" emerges which will indicate an appropriate ministry. When the storytelling/playhouse and naming/library church complement each other in an evolutionary cycle, together they facilitate the dawning of sacraments. The Rite of Christian Initiation for

Adults (RCIA) already models this happy alliance for us, naming God's children gracefully according to the stories they tell in the community.

Ministry and the Loss of Pastoral Innocence

Patterning the church and ecclesial ministry after the image of Jesus in overalls speaks of a conviction that order can be maintained in this life if sufficient effort is made. For many American Catholics a powerful challenge to this belief was issued by the experience of Vietnam. The lesson of that war was stark and brutal for those soldiers who went to fight with images of John Wayne and comic book superheroes in their heads. Their assumptions of victorious good guys and invulnerable heroes died a cruel death upon the alien soil of Vietnam. Their experience should be heeded by a church which seeks to minister to people in similar situations: "It's a jungle out there."

The film *Platoon* journals our national loss of innocence, the death in Vietnam of naive notions of life and country. Our orderly ministerial categories break down when we see soldiers murder innocent Vietnamese out of rage and frustration. Our convictions regarding the interplay of divine and human intervention are unsettled as we witness a young GI's agonizing journey to the decisive point of executing a murderous officer. Our confidence in rational response to crisis is shaken as we watch a commander order his air support to drop all remaining payloads on his own position during an ongoing battle where control and logic have long departed. I remember thinking after viewing the film that soldiers wear dog tags at war not so much to be identified by others after they are killed, but as a constant reference point for their own identities in the thick of the battle.

The gift of such stories is compassion, the ability to view a reality that is easily condemned from afar and see it in a new way. Indeed, the polarization between "hawks" and "doves" which splintered this nation during the sixties sounds a warning to a church torn by the warring of liberal and conservative factions. Maintenance ministry is about categorizing such experiences from a "control center" with a view toward an orderly and reasonable response. Storytelling ministry is about entering the story and sharing the journey so that our response becomes: "That could have been me!" or "That is me!" If we learn from such storytelling encounters that the world we live in does not always operate according to good housekeeping procedures, then we can shape our ministry accordingly. We then will have taken a vital step toward re-imagining our ministry for a messy world.

In *Ordinary People* the mother fired the maid because she couldn't dust the living room correctly. In an age when our ecclesial housekeepers like Bishop Hunthausen can be dismissed for improperly dusting our living room, such actions should give us pause. In a world where ministry takes place before the mess (the Garden), over the mess (God Almighty), against the mess (Jesus the Fixer), or after the mess (Ecclesial maintenance) such housekeepers should be fired. But in a messy world of ambiguity it seems we need all the help we can get. Most of all, we need those housekeepers who put down their feather-dusters in favor of hip-boots and jump with both feet into the graceful mess of human existence where the Body of Christ is daily being transfigured.

Items for Individual Reflection/Group Process

1. What are the roots of the church's desire to fashion a ministry geared toward keeping things under control and in order? What are the values of this approach? What are its pitfalls?

2. Has your desire for order in life been a liability to your loving acceptance of your children? Where do you draw the line between acceptance and control? Is it more important to you to "order your children" than to bless them? Does this priority transfer into other areas of ministry? How?

3. What would you identify as the primary mission of the church? What ties does that function have to the maintenance model of pastoral ministry?

4. Discuss the contrasting images of the church as "forest preserve" or "garden." What are your reactions to each? Consider the parable of the wheat and the weeds (Matt 13/24-30). Do you accept the Lord's decision to allow the weeds to remain amid the wheat or does this seem like a "mistake" to you?

5. What is your sense of the church as "light of the world"? In what ways, however subtle, do we still claim a monopoly on that light, a "corner on the market" (window)? How specifically can we burn in a way that calls people home instead of shutting them out (fireplace)?

6. What is the importance of naming in the life of the church? What are its limitations? Discuss the liturgical balance between the storytelling church (Liturgy of the Word) and the naming church (Liturgy of the Eucharist/Sacrament). How has past Catholic emphasis on Sacrament over Word been a liability to ministry in general? How has the church's reintegration of this "Protestant" orientation revitalized pastoral ministry?

7. Discuss the church's historical use of the term "Limbo." What did that word say about the people who were "placed there"? What did it say about us? Which people in the church today are still in Limbo? Why? Have you ever been "put in Limbo" by the church?

8. Consider the impact of the Vietnam war on the American church; on American society. How has that reality facilitated our loss of pastoral innocence? Has this been good or bad for America?; for the church? Explain.

Activities for Pastoral Staffs/Ministries

1. Have each member of the group write down their ideals about models of church ministry. Next, have individuals give each other feedback regarding how their pastoral styles actually come across. Learn from the agreements and discrepancies.

2. Review the assumptions and policies in your parish that effect maintenance procedures and personnel. These people facilitate ongoing ministry by doing the "behind the scenes" work. Do they have a forum for voicing their concerns? Are they appreciated? Are women still presumed to be responsible for volunteer cleanups, as reflected in a Sunday announcement like: "We need some women to clean the church?" Make whatever changes are suggested by these considerations. It might be beneficial to plan an appropriate celebration of housekeeping ministry and employees/volunteers.

3. Parish organizations might gather to develop strategies for making their ministries more responsive to an increasingly complex clientele. The fact is that what used to be the "abnormal" cases are fast becoming the norm (e.g., the numbers of children in a CCD program who have little idea what the catechist means when she refers to God as "a loving, ever present father"). What can be done to change the ground rules of our ministries so that such people can become "exceptional" rather than exiled to "Limbo"?

4. Ascertain the degree of honesty with which parish ministry is evaluated. In a recent "State of the Union" address, President Reagan thanked Nancy for helping turn the tide in the fight against drugs in the schools. This statement, uttered in the midst of an increasingly bleak forecast for the fight against drugs in this country, reflected a naivete that was detrimental to the struggle at hand. Is this kind of naivete a factor in your annual assessment of pastoral progress and need in your parish?

5. Analyze the balance in your worship between the liturgy of the Word (storytelling/playhouse) and the liturgy of the Eucharist or Sacrament (naming/library). Review the use of bells, your style of proclaiming the Word, the placement of the table and pulpit, etc. Make needed adjustments to acquire the balance that retains the integrity of both aspects of the liturgy.

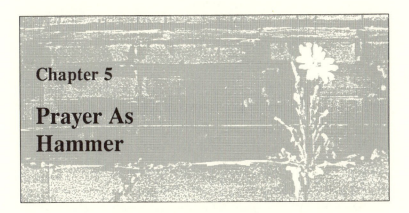

Chapter 5

Prayer As Hammer

"You can't always get what you want;
but if you try some time, you just might find you get what you need!"
— Jagger/Richards: "You Can't Always Get What You Want"

When I was a boy there was a very popular television show called "Whirly Birds." It was about two helicopter pilots who hired themselves out to various people in distress in order to save the day for them. My brother and I soon concluded that it was one of our favorite shows. Yet, like all true children, it was not enough for us just to watch; we had to get more personally involved. So, we used the back yard as our airfield and built two helicopters out of crates and boards.

After school, and before "Whirly Birds," we would spend hours flying around the neighborhood and other exotic locations doing deeds of heroism. Around dinner time our mother would come to the back door and order us to "come in for a landing" before supper. Reluctantly we would "turn off" the bent nails which formed the power switches on our choppers and prepare to go into the house. It was at this point that one of my earliest and clearest experiences of childhood prayer would begin.

I would usually stall for a few minutes so that my brother would return to the house first. Once alone I would sit back and begin to pray in a manner pretty close to this: "Okay, God, we're all alone now, nobody will see. Just give me one real trip over the neighborhood. I won't tell my brother or mother or anybody. You can even make me invisible if you're worried that I'll be seen. I know you can do it, God; I just know you can! Please!" Then, time after time, I would sit back with my eyes closed and my hope open. I would settle back and wait for...and wait for...and wait for...nothing. Somewhere along the line I gave up on that prayer. I "lost faith" and it died in me.

Learning Our Lessons About Prayer

Most of us grew up in the faith that "prayer is the answer." Yet, as someone wisecracked (wisely cracked open) one day: "Yes, but what was the question?" Or, to put it another way, "What kind of answer is prayer?" As Christians, we have available to us a wide variety of clues as to prayer's nature and purpose in Scripture, books, and homilies. Most of us, though, sort out the sticky business of prayer in the arena of our daily experience. The problem is that we don't always pay enough attention to that experience, are not nearly reflective enough about it, to grow in wisdom about prayer. Like the boy who misses his history lesson while daydreaming about his own heroic history of adventures, we are offered lessons about prayer every day in the school of experience but often prefer to daydream about what we would hope prayer to be for us.

It is this penchant of ours for ignoring the lessons of experience in favor of our "daydreams" that allows us to cling to unreal and unhelpful conceptions of prayer. Such unreal models of prayer do not die easily because they are so attractive in their promises. In my case, for example, while I came to that point where I no longer asked God to fly my helicopter, I simply "graduated" to more subtle forms of similar prayer. Perhaps they were made subtle to disguise their similarity to "the helicopter prayer" from me or from God.

The persistence of childish models of prayer in our lives can be explained partially by the great amount of reinforcement they received in our Christian upbringing. We certainly did not pick up our "great expectations" of prayer in a vacuum. The occasional arrival of a prayer chain letter in the mail or the discovery of a "prayer note" in a church pew indicates that such views of prayer are still with us. Above all, the rise of fundamentalism as a primary force in shaping American religious practices is a sign of the resilience of the human capacity to sustain childish prayer forms in the face of considerable evidence against their authenticity.

What we learned about prayer, very simply, is that it works. We came to appreciate prayer as the way to get what we want from God. Prayer for us became synonymous with asking. Our theology of prayer, regardless of how poetically we expressed it, often painted God as that great big vending machine in the sky. Prayer was the coin one had to insert in order to get the prize. Even selfless prayers sought some spiritual commodity for a temporal premium. The validity of this system was carefully founded in Scripture and corroborated by personal testimony.

A Pray-er's Rules of Order

Yet, the faithful were also taught that this divine vending machine system operated by certain rules. It was not all cut and dried for, after all, God is no pushover. Prayer is asking, to be sure ("Ask and you shall receive"; "How much more, then, will your Father in heaven give good things to those who ask?"), but there were conditions. This divine vending machine was somewhat touchy. One's prayer coin had to be inserted in just the right way or the prize one sought would not be forthcoming.

The first condition to the proper operation of the machine was faith: "If you believe, you will receive whatever you ask for in prayer." If we did not believe that our "God-machine" could deliver the prize we saw behind the glass window, it would not budge an inch, no matter how many prayer-coins we inserted. Secondly, we had to be persistent, like the widow in the Gospel story who got what she wanted from the judge because she bugged him to death. So, regardless of how many times our prayer-coin fell through the machine and landed in the coin return, we were required to patiently pick it up and reinsert it in the slot. Finally, we had to be putting the coin in the slot with the right intention, for the correct prize: "You do not have what you want because you do not ask God for it. And when you ask, you do not receive it, because your motives are bad; you ask for things to use for your own pleasures" (James 4/2-3). So, if we did not get the new bike we wanted for Christmas it was because we asked for something that "was not good for us."

Once we got the conditions down, however, our prayer life could move into high gear and really get things accomplished. We learned that our prayer life would help us against our enemies. The sign of the cross would certainly call down the divine powers to assist us in making a free throw. We never stopped to wonder why the opposition bothered with this gesture since God was obviously on our side (the Notre Dame syndrome). True to our Judaic roots, we also believed that God was behind the noble causes of our wars and would bring us through to victory. This deep seated belief is one of the reasons the Vietnam War was so hard on our national psyche. Again, we never stopped to consider the Lord's relationship to "the enemy."

Prayer also became for us a kind of armor against all sorts of evils: sickness, temptation, misfortune, and sin. I recall the "Mother of Perpetual Help" devotions of my youth. One regular feature of those novenas was the reading of a letter or two from people who had obtained such "miracles of protection" from their prayers to the Blessed Mother. These letters were followed by the reading of a list which gave an accounting, a kind of "spiritual spread sheet," of the numbers of cures, conversions, and other favors that were granted through Mary's intercession. Again, we were rarely very reflective about those cases in which prayer "failed" to avert some personal crisis. We held on to the belief that "prayer works" and we had the statistics to prove our hypothesis.

If accurately practiced, prayer would also provide answers to many of our spiritual questions; it would tell us what to do. What adult Christian has not at one time or another sought a solution to some crisis by letting the Bible randomly fall open and accepting the first passage to appear as "the answer to my prayer?" This practice often "worked" because Scripture stories have a universal quality which speaks to a wide variety of life experiences with a definite faith perspective. I remember that during the days of my novitiate I had a rather sophisticated system of signs which I would look for in order to make decisions about the direction of my life. It was the sincerity and seeming selflessness of such prayer which made it seem bonafide: "Whatever you want, God; all you have to do is show me the way."

Life Plays "Devil's Advocate"

However deeply entrenched were these convictions about the benefits of prayer, eventually they were bound to be challenged by the evidence of life experience. Even the stoutest fundamentalist must face the questions about prayer which life relentlessly asks. Why do good people die a hard death, despite their rosaries and novenas? Why do "the white hats" sometimes lose even the most noble struggles? Why do the innocent suffer at the hands of the guilty? So it was that our verdict about prayer as an access to a divine vending machine came under the gun of cross examination by ambiguous life experiences.

Now, it is possible to avoid hard questions and cling to "kinder" models of spirituality. In fact, it is quite normal for us as humans to hold on to existing faith paradigms for as long as possible. So it was that we were able to rationalize the contradictory evidence for a time and retain a belief in the kind of return we sought from the investment of our prayers. This rationale took the form of explaining away "failures" in prayer by citing failures in their preconditions. If a prayer was not answered it was due to a lack of faith, a faulty motive, insufficient persistence, or incorrect rubrics. If these explanations fell short we simply told ourselves that God's answer was "no."

The resurgence of fundamentalism is a symbol for the tenacity of such magical conceptions of prayer, a sign that they are still very much with us. Eventually, however, we must come to grips with the considerable problems presented by such models of spirituality. Chief among these is the image of God promoted by a "vending machine" theology of prayer. Let us consider the type of God we are left with if we retain such a model by taking the life of St. Monica as a case in point.

Monica is a classic model of the efficacy of prayer in that her persistent, faithful, and selfless petition effected the conversion of her son, Augustine. Yet, while we might properly be edified by such a story, we must also acknowledge the way it portrays God. We might imagine God up in heaven after Monica has been praying for years: "My, my, she certainly is a persistent one. I may have to take her seriously if she keeps this up much longer. Let's give her a while longer and then we'll see how confident she is."

We could also reflect upon the case of a cancer patient who, burdened with excruciating pain and dim forecasts for the future, angrily calls on God for some kind of relief. Again, we might imagine the vending machine God sticking that divine nose in the air and with folded arms pouting to Jesus: "He's gotta ask me nice!" Or we could focus on the dilemma of a woman who has suffered an incredible string of cruel misfortunes. Too discouraged and weary to summon much energy for prayer, her petition for help is tinged with doubt. Once more, our rationale for prayer gives us a picture of a God whose head is shaking sadly: "She doesn't really think I can do it. I'd like to help the poor lady out, but I'm afraid she'll have to get a little more pizazz into her prayer if she wants results."

If we are to hold on to the prayer of our youth, then, we must be prepared to accept with it a kind of God who is demanding and picky, if not downright snobbish and cruel. If, on the other hand, we desire to retain an image of God as intimately present and "full of kindness and fidelity," then we must also risk the abandonment of a style of prayer which has comforted us with its power and reliability. Such is the challenge and the choice which lies before us. Let us consider the possible shape of such a process of abandonment.

A New Physics for Prayer

If I were to describe the physics of the prayer I grew up with, its "flow chart" would look something like this:

a. prayer power goes up to heaven and "changes God" (impacts upon God with its faith and persistence and elicits a response);

b. prayer power then comes down to the world to change things (makes the world better, safer, healthier);

c. prayer power comes into me and changes me (the results of my prayer increase my faith energy and ready me to pray again).

This notion that prayer goes out from me in order to change the world is at the heart of "the helicopter prayer" I related earlier. Sitting on my helicopter I turned on a prayer switch which was intended to bring forth a reaction from God which would change my fake helicopter into a real one. Afterwards I would undoubtedly be much more excited about God, filled with faith, and eager to do the Lord's work in the world. Very simply, then, the "old prayer" changes God, who changes the world, which changes me.

Our reflection upon human experience, however, has revealed some of the peculiar difficulties of these prayer dynamics and invites us to explore new possibilities. Equipped with the knowledge provided by our ongoing reflection we might wet our finger and put it in the air for a more accurate sense of the dynamics of prayer. The new physics of prayer might yield a "flow chart" something like this:

a. prayer, as an interaction with God and the world, moves inward and changes me/us/the church (turns us, converts us);

b. prayer, as divine energy released from within me/us/the church through conversion, then moves outward to life and changes the world (makes it more compassionate, wise, whole);

c. prayer, as a force which shapes and realizes divine presence by its efficacy, moves "upward" and "changes God" (makes the Lord more present, visible, active, incarnate in our eyes).

But in order to dispel any fears that what I am suggesting implies that prayer does not work, it may be helpful to summarize this model in another way:

1. Does prayer make things happen? Yes! Prayer makes things happen.

2. Does prayer make things happen by activating and focusing divine power? Yes! Prayer summons and applies divine power.

3. Does prayer make things happen by summoning power which is absent or conditional, held back by God in a secret storehouse, from a divine world into a human world? No! Prayer works by calling forth powers and gifts that are already ours through Creation and reaffirmed through the Incarnation.

The third point makes all the difference!

This has been the basic conversion I have experienced in my prayer life. I was taught and happily accepted the notion that prayer was a hammer ("If I Had A Hammer") I could use to reshape human existence so that I could be happier in order to do God's work. The more I "grew up," the more problems and frustrations I experienced trying to use prayer in that way. I slowly yielded to life's hard lesson: prayer simply does not change life in the manner I learned and hoped it would. In occasional crises I continue to revert to that model of prayer, trying to force it to "get my way," but in the end I grow more frustrated and unhappy.

Prayer is indeed a hammer, but the hammer works first on us. We then become a hammer to work at reshaping human existence and grow happier as God is made increasingly present for all in that process. So now I find that I very rarely pray for things "to happen" outside of my relationship to those events as an evolving whole. I see that prayer gradually opens us up to what happens instead of helping us compulsively seek to make things happen the way we want. This frees us to rely more on our inner resources (charisms) and those of the community (the indwelling Spirit), discovered through the power of prayer to shape them, to obtain what we need to be the Lord's creative force (ministers) in life.

Prayer as "Talking to Ourselves"

In Alice Walker's book, *The Color Purple*, Celie experiences a similar conversion. Her letter prayers are addressed to God until mounting tragedy leads to a faith crisis: "Dear Nettie, I don't write to God no more, I write to you." She defends her decision to her friend, Shug, who is trying to point out God's kindness toward her: "Yeah,...and he give me a lynched daddy, a crazy mama, a lowdown dog of a step pa, and a sister I probably won't ever see again. Anyhow,...the God I been praying and writing to is a man. And act just like all the other mens I know. Trifling, forgitful, and lowdown."

Yet, in the end Celie comes full circle. Her final letter is addressed once again to God (and everything). What she finds is the vital link between prayer and people and life itself. She thought she had stopped praying, but she had really only begun to "pray to people," to find the God she lost in her sister, her friends, herself, and even those who had done harm to her. She abandons dualistic prayer in favor of creationist prayer. Shug capsulizes her journey: "Here's the thing,...The thing I believe. God is inside you and inside everybody else. You come into the world with God. But only them that search for it inside find it. And sometimes it just manifest itself even if you not looking, or don't know what you looking for. Trouble do it for most folks, I think. Sorrow, lord. Feeling like shit."

So, while I continue to "visit him" at times, I find for the most part that I am no longer the little boy sitting on the makeshift helicopter, waiting for God to finally come through with the miraculous wonder of "real flight." Admittedly, there is a certain sadness in that passage. Yet, on the other hand, I also have discovered a formerly untapped ability to "fly away" in my imagination. I have learned that the gifts we seek are ours for the making if only we can stop looking for them in the precise ways we want. If we allow our prayer to "come in" and open us up to life, our dreams and imagination can open up new worlds, can change the world with their creative power.

It is that "new world," the product of our prayer, in which God is truly found. It seems to me that such a use of prayer is an authentic ground for ministry. Before going on to a more detailed exploration of how that ministry might look, however, it seems appropriate to examine one more area of our life as church, the expression of public worship which we call liturgy.

Items for Individual Reflection/Group Process

1. The story of "the helicopter prayer" relates a childhood experience which outlines a model for prayer (how it works; what it is for). Recall an early prayer experience of your own and trace the presumptions about prayer it contained.

2. Does the author's "flow chart" of the physics of prayer seem consistent with your faith?; with your experience? What do you make of the suggestion that prayer influences people rather than God (it affects people which effects God)?

3. The author agrees that prayer changes things, but argues that this happens because people are moved by prayer (moved into action) rather than God being moved (talked into something she wasn't originally interested in). Do you accept this, or do you see a need to maintain a direct link between the action of personal prayer and the reaction of the Lord?

4. Recall the conditions for effective prayer: faith, perseverance, right intention. How do these qualities square with the notion that prayer changes us before it changes God (makes God more present to people)? What part would these qualities play within the new physics of prayer suggested here? What purpose would they serve in effecting a "pray-er life"?

5. How do you account for the experience of not getting what you pray for? What do these breakdowns in prayer mean for a theology which sees prayer as influencing God? What are the ramifications for a type of prayer that is seen as moving people?

6. If prayer is truly for people and reaps benefits as it impacts upon them through the action of the Spirit, how might we reformulate our reasons for engaging in the various types of prayer? What might be the particular benefits of rote prayer, group prayer, meditation, public worship, etc. according to the new dynamics of prayer outlined here?

7. How has the experience of Vietnam affected our prayer life as Americans? We grew up with the concept that God was "on our side" (as evidenced by our free-throw prayers at basketball games). How has our feeling of losing the Vietnam War challenged forms of prayer which presume "good guys always win"? How does prayer change when we are shocked into considering the Lord's presence among "the enemy"?

8. What sort of prayer model is expressed in your parish's Sunday liturgy? Do your petitions tend to pray for things to change or for people to be converted and activated? Which emphasis do you prefer and how can it be achieved in your prayer?

Activities for Pastoral Staffs/Ministries

1. Periodically parish staffs and ministries could follow up a normal prayer experience with a reflection This exercise should be spontaneous so that participants will not be overly conscious of performance while they pray. What dynamics of prayer are operational in the way you pray as a group? What is the power of your prayer?; what are its weaknesses? Does your prayer reflect the dynamics of prayer discussed above?

2. Identify the priorities of your group/parish prayer. What do you pray for the most? the least? What is the balance (or imbalance) of prayer and action in your group/parish? What changes are suggested?

3. Develop strategies for the maturing of community prayer. Does parish prayer, for example, tend to be very "myopic"? Choose appropriate means for stimulating growth in the prayer life of the people: bulletin articles, homilies, Lenten programs, days or evenings of prayer, etc.

4. Meet with whatever prayer groups are functioning in the parish or community. Begin the delicate process of supporting and challenging such groups as necessary. A starting point might be occasional staff presence at prayer group meetings. If any practices need to be confronted, this should be done gently, but firmly. Perhaps all such groups could be integrated into an overall parish/community prayer ministry which would gather for input, celebration, and fellowship at regular intervals.

5. Write down your dreams and wishes. Divide them into the categories of needs (things people have to have) and wants (things people would like to have). Which do you pray for most often? Reflect on the need for conversion in your prayer life?

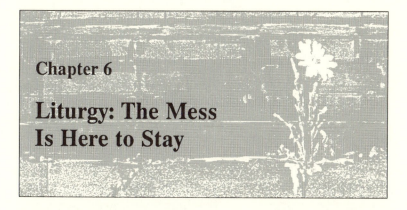

Chapter 6

Liturgy: The Mess Is Here to Stay

She say, "Celie, tell the truth, have you ever found God in church? I never did. I just found a bunch of folks hoping for him to show. Any God I ever felt in church I brought in with me. And I think all the other folks did too. They come to church to share God, not find God."
— Alice Walker: *The Color Purple*

There are certain events in life, the significance and impact of which are verified by the fact that people recall exactly where they were and what they were doing when the incident occurred. One such event in recent years was the assassination attempt on the life of the Pope. I vividly recall sitting at my desk in my religious education office when the news of the shooting was announced over the intercom. I sat there and listened to the many questions and feelings that resonated within my silence. In the days that followed I also sensed the import of the event for the people in the community.

The shooting had hit the parish hard because of the many implications it held for the state of the world and the direction human life was taking.

The liturgy for the Sunday which followed the shooting is also very clear in my mind. That Mass was the liturgical counterpart of what a religious educator would call "a teachable moment." The Eucharists of that weekend were "prayable moments" because they held the potential to process hopes and fears that were very keenly present in the faith lives of the participants, to send up a cry for divine assistance that would never be more authentic or heartfelt.

The Gospel for that Sunday, fittingly enough, dealt with faith amid adversity. I recall it as the story of Jesus calming the storm at sea. The homily followed a very familiar pattern, rallying the people to the strong faith that was billed as the key to successfully navigating the current crisis. The goal was to assure people that God's love and power would prevail, that the Lord would reassert control despite our fears of impending chaos. While this is certainly a legitimate approach to such a situation, it didn't seem to address the community's faith in the context of the real life situation at hand.

During the week I had been personally coming to terms with the issues raised by the shooting. Out of that reflection and prayer a song emerged which seemed to say something honest about my "faith status" and that of the community in light of what had taken place. On Sunday I had the refrain printed on the back of the

weekly songsheet and after communion the choir led
the people in sharing that prayer. Here are some of the
words:

> Look all around and see what I've found:
> Confusion and pain and despair.
> We all try to cope; we know there's still hope;
> The question we're asking is "where?"
>> Be with us, Lord, be with us.
>> Please do not leave us alone.
>> Be with us, Lord, be with us.
>> Walk with us on our way home.
> Many a heart broken apart;
> Many a life sinking low.
> Where will it end? Where did it begin?
> Tell us, Lord, must it be so?

As I looked out over the people while we were singing
this song, as I heard their voices and saw their tears, I
felt that something real and important had taken place
at that liturgy. Somehow our prayer that day had
confronted and processed a mess rather than explaining
it away. We had taken a step toward authentic belief
within a messy world rather than engaging in a
repressive exercise which projected an ideal faith
beyond it.

Liturgy:
"The Medium is the Message"

This is a pivotal chapter in these writings. The first
part of this book has focused on a review of our

111

expectations of God and Jesus and how those expectations have formed our beliefs and ecclesial ministry. We have asked questions about how real life experiences may inform and reshape our faith. Now we must turn our attention more specifically to the ministerial implications of faith's expectations once they have been exposed to a hard look at life as it is experienced by the people of God.

I have chosen liturgy as the focus for this chapter precisely because ritual acts as a fulcrum in our life of faith for just such an endeavor. Liturgy expresses the type of faith we bring to it and nourishes such faith toward a new and more authentic expression in the context of life. In short, our rituals do exactly what this book is intended to do: it speaks of where we have come from and points the way to where we are going. Liturgy graciously celebrates the past even as it urges us to let go and invite the future.

It was Marshal McLuhan who announced the truth that "the medium is the message." So it is that the way we do liturgy reflects the state of our faith. To study liturgical history is to review a map of how we have forged our way over the terrain of life. Ritual is a diary of the journey of faith. More vital to our purposes, though, is how the modern liturgical renewal mirrors our communal journey from belief in a tidying grace to faith in a graceful mess.

One goal of pre-Vatican II liturgy was to create a neat and ethereal utopia, an escape from "the world." While contemporary worship may need to reclaim some lost sense of mystery and "the beyond" from that era, we cannot lose sight of the distortions which Tridentine liturgy perpetuated. Those who long to return to the liturgical "good old days" often retain the following conception of its merits:

1. It gave us a breather from the rigors of life's messiness.

2. It provided the grace to survive our reentry into the messy world without undue contamination.

3. It reminded us that our ultimate goal in life was complete escape from the finite world and elevation into that orderly kingdom of which the liturgy was a pale image.

The look and feel of the post-Vatican II liturgy, on the other hand, is entirely different. Our renewed liturgy challenges us to enter the world and celebrate the grace discovered therein. Post Vatican II liturgy ritualizes our newfound belief that the mess is here to stay and that the Lord's truest glory is revealed there. Sunday Mass asks us to celebrate our encounters rather than our escapes, to share divine energy rather than take it, and to invest ourselves in making the Kingdom happen rather than merely surviving until the Kingdom happens to us.

To clarify just how deeply the renewed liturgy has come to model these new convictions and challenges, we shall spend some time reviewing the key paradigm shifts in church worship since Vatican II. These capsule studies reveal just how much the new liturgy is coming to look and feel like real life. Such reflections will also suggest directions for further liturgical renewal and will serve as a fitting lead-in to a focus in the pages that follow on the shape of effective ministry in a messy world.

Sacrament:
Saving Grace to Messy Salvation

The purpose of the sacraments has changed, or at least expanded. If we were to simplify our past sense of these rites, we might be left with a caricature highly associated with order and neatness. We were baptized to be cleaned up and transformed into children of God. When we had the messy stain of Original Sin on our souls we were unfit for the indwelling of the Spirit. Yet, a little water and a few words rendered us spotless and worthy of membership in God's family. Because we were so prone to messiness this state of purity was fragile, but we had the sacrament of Penance to help us with spot cleanups. Confirmation made us soldiers of Christ so that we could go out and battle the forces of chaos. Eucharist permitted us a sampling of the bread of angels. Matrimony allowed us to breathe a little easier by legitimizing and controlling the sexual activity of a couple. Holy Orders provided us with those who could "step up higher" and mediate the orderly world to the corrupted one. Extreme Unction gave us the comfort of a final checkup before facing God.

The evolution of sacramental practice from the early church came to effect and model evolving theologies about their purpose. An immersion of adults into a pool, and so into the mystery of life in Christ, became a dripping of water to rescue and shield pagan infants from corruption. Confirmation oil which once flowed down foreheads like the gracious, embarrassing Spirit of God came to be wiped up by attendants, implying the virtues of controlling our prophetic Spirit. The Bread of Life which was first shared as "real food," the product of community, was later mass produced into tasteless wafers, teaching us that "communion" happens through the efficient distribution of a product. The magical overtones which came to characterize many of these rites further extolled human passivity and convenience.

Our children celebrate a different brand of sacraments. Baptism is an affirmation of their status as children of God despite the messiness of their existence. Christians enter the water to commit themselves to the journey rather than to escape it and many of them are getting wet in the process. Confirmation oil now drips from the foreheads of our Confirmandi, inviting them to "go with the flow" of their life in the Spirit. Bread baking ministries are common in parishes, a sign that "communion" is the product of an impractical investment of human resources in each other and in the Lord. Priests/Ministers are now being ordained to be with people rather than above them and to affirm gifts that are already present in the community. The Anointing of The Sick is not a "final preparation for takeoff" but a sign of healing power and presence even as the journey goes on.

Yet, the old ways of our liturgical conditioning do not die easily. We have the new wine of revised rites, but often the old wineskins of liturgical ministers remain unchanged. Recently I heard of an Easter Vigil which the pastor introduced with a long discourse on the messy perils of candles, the proper way to hold them to avoid dripping wax, and the wisdom of keeping them out of children's hands. A few years ago I planned a children's service that resulted in excitement and participation at the expense of noisiness. Immediately upon the conclusion of this liturgy the principal strode to the front of the church and conducted a "kneeler practice" which involved children putting kneelers up and down quietly several times. The underlying messages of these actions are certainly not lost upon people. They soon learn to be reserved, stiff, and on guard rather than energetic, open, and at home during ritual.

The greatest discovery of the new liturgy, however, is the revelation that we are not given sacraments as possessions but that we must live sacraments as commitments. We must be sacraments in the context of community. The revitalization of the RCIA, and the modeling of all other sacramental activity after it, is the key to a messier ecclesial future in which people discover community as the basic sacrament: "The most powerful experience of the sacred is found in the celebration and the persons celebrating, that is, it is found in the action of the assembly..." ("Environment and Art in Catholic Worship"). The resurgence of the

Catechumenate and the rise of base communities will make for a less controlled and tidy, but more rewarding and graceful, life in the church.

Environment:
Linear Power to Circular Power

Modern adults who attended parish worship as youths quickly caught on that learning to go church meant learning how to "stay in line" both literally and figuratively. Indeed, the line was the central organizing factor in the creation of an environment that was very neat, categorized, and controlled. The line of the communion rail separated the sanctuary from the nave. The assembly sat in lines called pews, processed in lines, and knelt in a line to receive communion. In short, the creed of the pre- Vatican II liturgy implicitly held that communion (community) is accomplished most effectively when people do not "step out of line."

This linear organization was vital, not only to preserving the neatness of the liturgical world, but to categorizing every faction of the liturgy according to another type of line called a "plane," a level of existence. The communion rail was important because it kept the sanctuary, the place where God finds refuge, apart from the nave, the place where the tainted laity dwells. Only at communion time could the common masses approach the holy place to receive their taste of the divine. The priest on the altar said Mass from a higher plane and the choir took residence up in the loft, a privilege obtained by their usurpation of the higher art of music from the people down below. The underlying assumption for this geometrical world, of course, was the belief that such an environment was more conducive to the flow of grace.

The new liturgy proclaims our faith in the Lord whose life travels in circles (note that "going around in circles" is usually a metaphor for confusion and ineffectiveness). In other words, the grace of the Lord is in a sense unorganized, spontaneous, free-flowing, and uncontrollable. This discovery is reflected in the environmental changes in the liturgy. Communion rails have been dismantled and lines of pews have been reshaped into circles. Priests and choirs have come down off their planes and now are incorporated into the circle of the community. The whole liturgical action has shifted from the notion of lining up to that of gathering. We believe that God is made present and active in such untidy surroundings.

Ministry:
Doing For to Doing With

No one would put up much of an argument with the claim that things seem much simpler when you can have someone else do them for you. Pre-Vatican II liturgy was built on the premise that the laity simply needed to show up and sit in the pews in order to receive the necessary graces to survive in a messy and Godless world. Even the priest, who operated as a one man ministerial army at Mass, was viewed as merely an instrument of the workings of God. It was understood that anyone else involved in the Mass was simply the priest's helper, just as the priest was God's helper.

In fact, if there is an image which might capture the ministerial dynamics of the pre-Vatican II liturgy, it would be the process of getting a sun tan. When a sun-worshipper goes to the beach to "catch some rays," the role of the other people who provide services is secondary. The lifeguard (priest), the vendor (Eucharistic minister), the radio disc jockey (choir), and the security personnel (ushers) all have a function and are welcome extras, but they are not directly involved with the success or failure of getting a tan. So, those who have taken on ministerial roles in the renewed liturgy have inherited a mission long regarded as expendable from a spiritual standpoint. Anyone who has struggled to convince a passive assembly of the importance of their participation knows how strong our faith in human superfluity has been. In the beach model of liturgical ministry, only an "act of God" like inclement weather can prevent the Son's power from getting through.

A more appropriate image for revealing the role of the post- Vatican II liturgical minister would be that of a baseball game (if we take care not to reduce the mystery of God to this event). In that setting the power and life which the participants seek is released only through the cooperation of all the "ministers" involved. If any of them fail to do their part, power is lost and the quality of the experience suffers. Picture a home run without the cheers of the "assembly" or the effect of a mediocre team effort on the enthusiasm of the crowd. Think of a ballgame lacking the symbolic food of a hotdog or without the ritual of a vendor selling them. Imagine the cheers of the crowd without the organist to initiate those cheers and give them life. Think of the confusion and resentment caused by discourteous ushers or the absence of ushers when they are needed. Such is the importance of liturgical ministers to the success of the post-Vatican II liturgy. Where once only an act of God could short circuit the flow of power, now human acts can as well.

Feasts:
A Clean Getaway to a Clumsy Entrance

One way of understanding the values of an institution or a people is to examine their calendar of holidays. When you see what they celebrate you have a clue as to what is important to them. If neutral observers were to go over our calendar of feast days with a sense of their meaning for us, they might well come away with the conclusion that we value protection from the world or total escape from it above all else. The Immaculate Conception, the Virgin Birth, All Saints, Easter, and the Ascension all rejoice in events which speak of purity from, victory over, or escape from the world. Now, while these feasts need not be interpreted in such a fashion, the celebration of "a clean getaway" from the world was a quite common way of viewing them.

In their book, *How to Save the Catholic Church*, Andrew Greely and Mary Durkin Greely speak of the good faith sense of the people which is drawing us back toward the Incarnation as the favorite and central feast of the Catholic imagination. One could certainly question whether Christmas needs to be named as "central," but the argument that its popular appeal has stymied our efforts to place Easter at the forefront of Christian consciousness certainly has weight.

Possibly the lesson here is that people desperately need to celebrate the presence of the divine in the midst of their messy existence (a clumsy entrance like the Incarnation) more than they need to rejoice that "someday" we will be victorious over death (often the limited, but popular "clean getaway" conception of the Resurrection). More and more the focus of the liturgy has become a celebration of the mysteries of God as they apply to life here and now, as they point the way toward life in the midst of death. This is the reason, for example, behind the wisdom of proclaiming that it is impossible to celebrate Easter without taking part in the Triduum, that there are no "clean getaways" without "clumsy entrances." The glory of Holy Week is fully discovered by those who enter by way of inconvenient and "clumsy" liturgical moments like Palm Sunday processions. The renewed liturgy celebrates festivals of a God who enters our mess rather than escaping it.

Consciousness:
Left Brain to Right Brain

The logical mind of "Star Trek's" Spock would find comfort in many aspects of our liturgy. Pre-Vatican II worship deserves its part of the blame because of its organizing structure and pragmatic symbols. Yet, Vatican II shares responsibility for the continuation of left-brained liturgy. In some respects the use of the vernacular and the creation of superfluous ministries has added fuel to the fire of our love affair with logic. The introduction of English allowed us to attach themes to our Masses and to appoint commentators to provide the assembly with a running commentary of the action. The banner, a by-product of liturgy committees, gave us an opportunity to put all kinds of words up in public for our minds to ponder. Even the privilege of hearing the Gospel in English prompted many to use homily time to explain the story again as if we were not quite capable of catching it on our own in one hearing.

We are just now beginning to take seriously the challenge of giving our right brains a little exercise at liturgy. This is a difficult challenge to accept because it involves letting go of control over the logistics of worship. It invites us to give our logical minds a break, becoming less "theo-logical," and to open up our intuitive selves. It asks that we take art seriously and utilize our artists. It begs us to forestall a consumer approach to liturgy which fills every precious silent space with spiritual commodities. The outward appearance may be one of chaos. Yet, when we allow symbols to speak, spark religious imagination, make spaces where there once were only words, and balance intellect with emotion, we actually gain a great deal more influence over the release of the experience of God.

Grace:
Cheap Grace to Getting What You Pay For

Grace was so appealing when it was cheap, easy to come by. See the pastor a few times and be baptized, say certain prayers correctly and gain an indulgence, go through some formalities and get married, attend the parish school and be escorted to church for Lenten Reconciliation. It was so easy then. Grace was a commodity, an item "for sale" at every local church for a very reasonable price. This is why Catholic school parents today often complain of "not getting their money's worth" for tuition when new sacramental programs demand their involvement.

Prior to Vatican II we spawned a race of bargain hunters for grace. It should come as no surprise to us that the creation of programs and processes which make grace accessible in an entirely different manner has caused many of those people to go shopping for parishes which "make grace the old fashioned way," which to their religious mentality is surely not "to earn it." The arguments for cheap grace are varied, subtle, and alluring: "God gives grace freely, nothing is required"; "If we don't take them to the sacraments they won't go"; "What good does it do to make people do things they really aren't interested in?"

There is a scene in the movie *The Mission* in which the mercenary played by Robert DeNiro is doing penance for killing his brother. His penance requires him to drag a heavy bundle of the tools of his trade, armor and weapons, up a mountain to the mission. After a long and arduous trek, one of the Jesuits begs the leader to put and end to the punishment: "He's done this penance long enough; and, well, the other brothers think the same." The priest's reply is simple: "But he doesn't think so, John; and until he does, neither do I."

So it is that our commitment to grace that "gives what is paid for" will demand a great price. We will have to spend more time with people, we will lose some because of our demands, we will have to respond to people as individuals, we will need to pay attention to the quality of our programs. Most of all, according to the wisdom of the RCIA, we will have to learn to be church in an entirely different way. In the end, the effort will be worth it in terms of the quality of the grace that is released. The renewed liturgy rejects the neat and simple path toward cheap grace in favor of the rugged journey toward getting the grace that we pay for.

Church:
Self-Centered to Universal Church

Matt Fox, in his book *The Coming of the Cosmic Christ*, warns us of becoming too anthropocentric in our spirituality. Worship can benefit by our specific application of his call for a return to a universal church (a church of the universe) as opposed to a church that is self-centered, trapped in a narcissistic focus on humanity alone. Our worship will be well served by an awareness of the awe and limitlessness of the cosmos, that sense of worship reflected in the Sanctus. That hymn moves us beyond a puny focus on individual or local concerns to an awe-full appreciation of our solidarity in praise with the entire universe: "Heaven and earth are full of your glory!"

In this light it might be advantageous to expand the wisdom of the liturgical document on Art and Environment which reads: "The most powerful experience of the sacred is found in the celebration and the persons celebrating, that is, it is found in the action of the assembly..." Perhaps what is called for is an expansive vision of liturgy rather than a reductionist one. Such a vision would suggest that the most powerful experience of the sacred is found when the entire cosmos is gathered to worship, when we are aware of the immensity, the mystery, and the wonder of the God that we celebrate rather than the smallness of our own private world.

Spirituality:
Ideal Selves to Real Selves

In view of all that has been said in this chapter, perhaps no call is more vital to the future development of liturgy than that of allowing our true selves to shine forth in liturgical worship. Maybe in the past we have exercised a great deal of repression in ritualizing our faith through our ideal selves rather than as the people we really are. Perhaps we have been far too nice to God by hiding many of our negative feelings and covering them with expressions of false piety. Bearing in mind that liturgy is concerned with expressing our truest and future selves, we might benefit from an investigation into the healthiness of a bit more humanity and honesty in our ritual.

Look through a Christian hymnal and count the hymns that express faith, praise, trust, and thanks. Then page through it again and number the hymns which manifest any of the doubt, anger, fear, or desperation that are so characteristic of real human life. Examine the Sunday Lectionary to see the number of readings which reflect the kind of anguished searching which Job experienced. How many prayers from the Sacramentary speak of the more human side of life? How many homilies come forth from throats which sound as if the life has been gargled out of them with theological mouthwash?

Perhaps we need to fashion our liturgical prayer in the mold of the psalmist who was able to yell at and question God as a way of once more coming around to express an underlying trust and love. We have many songs which express noble sentiments like "Be Not Afraid", and that is as it should be. Maybe we need a few more hymns which say "Lord, We Are Afraid." I wonder if just once in a while the lector should approach the podium and, rather than beginning his orderly list of prepared petitions, begin banging on the podium while crying out: "God help us! We hurt!"

Certainly I would not be calling for the liturgy to become some sort of ecclesial sensitivity session in which the faithful "let it all hang out" before the Lord. Some of this facet of ritual may be more appropriate to small group process, what Tad Guzie refers to as "micro church liturgy," as opposed to the "macro church" worship that takes place on Sunday. Yet, if the liturgy has begun to be the medium which is the message that we live in a different world, a messier world than the one in which many of us grew up, it seems that our prayer must assume some of that honesty in its formulation. If everything about our worship has become less tidy and more challenging, the culmination of that renewal may involve taking the risk of showing our real selves before God and community, not just the ideal selves we so often reveal. The Vietnam War Memorial in Washington D.C. is a paradigm of how such "ugly symbols" bring healing through their ritualization of messy human realities. It is just this kind of symbol, if introduced into Christian liturgy more freely, might work wonders through "faith-healings" of human brokenness.

We have spent a good deal of time looking at our faith in terms of the messiness of human experience. Now it is time to turn our attention to the type of ministry which emerges once we admit to ourselves and God that life is much messier than we might wish it to be. We shall now address the question of what type of ministry is adequate to respond to the realization that life is indeed very messy, to the messiness of life itself.

Items for Individual Reflection/Group Process

1. Review the many ways that the liturgical world before Vatican II served as a symbol of the way we wished the world to be and a protection against the way the world "out there" really was. How have the liturgical changes symbolized a new world and a new agenda for liturgical action?

2. Discuss the ways that modern sacraments have grown less neat and practical. What challenges have been met in this exodus from saving grace to messy salvation? What work remains?

3. We long presumed that divine power was transmitted in lines (by staying in line), but we now realize that grace "goes around in circles." What does this say about the world and how God operates in it? What does it indicate about ministry?

4. Consider the two models of the liturgical experience as contrasted in this chapter. The image of going to the beach, it is claimed, has given way to an image of experiencing a ball game. What are the implications for liturgical ministry in this shift?; for ministry in general? In what ways do we still prefer "getting a tan" to getting involved in the game?

5. Look over the church calendar. What is it that you ritualize on each of the feasts of the liturgical year? Do you tend to celebrate "clean getaways" (someday I'll be happy; I'll escape this "valley of tears") or "clumsy entrances" (God is here in the mess; true glory comes out of engagement, not escape)?

6. Review your personal prayer life (especially meditation). Do you use prayer as a rational exercise to figure faith out? Do you feel impelled to use worship as an opportunity to teach religion (explain symbols, instill themes, reinforce lessons)? How might we allow liturgy to embrace our right-brains?

7. What are you willing to pay for grace? What are we prepared to "charge" each other for grace? In what ways does our hesitation to put an end to cheap grace stem from misconceptions of Christians as "nice" and God as "gracious" (giving divine life away for free)?

8. What are your feelings about liturgy as a medium which speaks your full and honest self? Is there a need for more honest human expression at liturgy (grief, fear, doubt)? How might this be accomplished in a sensitive and faith-full manner?

9. How does your parish deal with the "messiness" that often characterizes Sunday liturgy: latecomers, crying infants, early departures, etc.? How can we remain sensitive to the disorder in people's lives without allowing it to unduly disrupt the liturgical experience?

Activities for Pastoral Staffs/Ministries

1. Reflect together on the power of the Vietnam War Memorial to ritualize the brokenness of the veterans and their families. A copy of the book *The Wall* might be obtained so that its photos could illustrate the healing that has been wrought through this "ugly" memorial. What ugly symbols of human brokenness are needed in your parish/community liturgy to ritualize and heal wounded faith?

2. Parish staffs might review liturgical ministry to see to what extent a housekeeping mentality has been an obstacle to good ritual. Review the structure of the church, the arrangement of furniture, the use of artificial candles, flowers, and greens, the generosity with which symbols are used, the roles of liturgical ministers, the incorporation of women into the liturgy, the perception of priests as "celebrants," and the value of current worship aids. Decide in which cases change is necessary because "cleanliness is removed from Godliness."

3. Gather the First communion staff and teachers together as the time for the celebration draws near. Reflect back on the rehearsal from the previous year to identify what values took up the most time and energy. Was appearance of primary concern (a left-brained desire to have the children look good in the way they move and act); or was impression the chief goal (a right-brained value for the feeling, the lasting sense of the occasion that the children come away with)? Clarify your values and plan the rehearsal accordingly.

4. Evaluate parish/community sacramental ministry in terms of our former "indelible mark" theology. Is sacramental preparation carried out in a token and convenient way, which implies that sacraments are automatic and indelible (we can't lose them), or is there a care and investment that marks sacraments as fragile (grace can be lost, squandered)? Particular attention might be paid to divorce ministry (those whose experience teaches us that

grace can be lost), to challenging consumer attitudes that claim a right to sacraments based on tuition payments rather than personal presence, and to the practice of videotaping sacraments (the illusion that we permanently capture grace on film rather than temporarily—temporally/in time—releasing it by human participation).

5. Evaluate your methods of sacramental preparation for those who do not fit into neat categories: children of inactive parishioners, RCIA candidates who show up "at the wrong time," etc. Are such people sometimes squeezed into existing slots for the sake of convenience? Make adjustments in your programs to accomodate these people's messy needs.

PART TWO

GOING TOWARD MINISTRY AS INCARNATION

"Then God said: 'Let there be light!' "
— Genesis 1/3

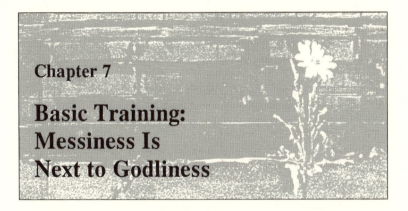

Chapter 7

Basic Training:
Messiness Is
Next to Godliness

"I had a tank of tropical fish. Someone turned up the tank heater
and they all boiled...It looked like violence, but it was such a quiet
night. And I remember wishing I had the kind of ears that could
hear fish screams because they looked as if they had suffered and I
wanted so badly to save them. That Sunday in church I heard that
Christ told his apostles to be fishers of men. From then on I looked
at all the people in the church as fish and so I knew that they were
all quiet screamers. Church was so quiet. And I thought everyone
was boiling. And I wanted the kind of ears that could hear what they
were screaming about, because I wanted to save them."
— Bill Davis: *Mass Appeal*

In the film *Whose Life Is It Anyway?*, Richard
Dreyfuss plays Ken Harrison, a gifted artist who is
rendered a quadriplegic by an auto accident. The movie
chronicles his struggles to deal with his condition and
those of a hospital staff to minister to him. Eventually
the artist arrives at the decision to put a halt to the

treatment that is keeping him alive. He argues for the "right to die" because life itself is more of a torment to him than the prospect of death. He has lived life so vigorously that his vibrant spirit is being tortured by the prison of a lifeless body. His physicians spend much of the film trying to convince him to go on living. They see his potential, despite its limitations, and the value of the life that possesses it.

In one scene the patient is particularly agitated and a doctor comes in to give him a sedative. This conversation ensues:

Doctor: "Here, I think this will help you."

Harrison: "Don't do that! Don't give me that!"

Doctor: "Why not? It will make you feel better."

Harrison: "Quieter you mean."

Doctor: "Look, Mr. Harrison, your body cannot handle all this excitement. Now, I think you need this."

Harrison: "Why?

If I want to be mad, I'll be mad.

If I want to make noise, I'll make noise.

You know, just because you are all so upset because you can't do anything for me doesn't mean that I'm the one who has to get tranquilized!" The only thing that I have left is my consciousness and I don't want that paralyzed as well. So if you want any tranquility, you eat the pill!"

Ministry: Tranquility or Tranquilizer

It is not my intent here to argue the moral issues raised by this encounter. I am more interested in the ministerial bias we bring to such situations and develop as a result of them. If we are to minister in a messy world, we must take time to train in the places where things are very hard. We cannot be credible in offering life to the living if we have not learned its value amid the dying and pleaded its case to those who feel dead. In our responses to the people and situations where life is messiest we get a sense of our modus operandi as ministers in those circumstances. We might consider whether we have preserved our self image as effective physicians at the expense of the wounded by dispensing ministerial tranquilizers. Like the doctor in the story above, have we quieted the questions and emotions of the suffering through the use of pious rationalizations because we seek tranquility in the face of our own pastoral limitations and those of God? Is the best barometer of effective ministers their response to the situations where they "can't do anything"?

Since life is the bootcamp in which our basic training for ministry takes place, an answer to these questions may lie in a review of our ministerial responses according to the categories introduced in the first half of the book. Such a review will reveal that we do have pastoral options when we are faced with a mess and that the course of action chosen is often determined by how

life is defined or categorized. Let us take a brief look at
the kind of minister and ministry produced by either our
denial or acceptance of life as messy.

Life in Eden
vs.
Life in a Messy World

The minister who regards the spotlessness and order
of Eden as the first goal of ministry simply cannot allow
a mess to exist. The minister molded according to this
pattern must always be repelled by the messiness of
human existence and dedicated to cleaning it up at all
costs. The energies of such a person are not dispensed
on people, but on the ugliness which needs to be
cleaned up at all costs. The minister, however, who
regards life as imperfect, sin as truly "Original" rather
than as spilled milk, realizes that messiness is normal.
Such a person expects people and situations to be
messy. The authentic minister is drawn to life's
messiness as the place "where the action is" and
employs a personal style of ministry toward "ugly"
individuals out of a conviction of their inherent beauty
as God's children.

To understand the difference here we might compare
ministry to allowance. A few years ago one of our sons
approached my wife and informed her that he had two
weeks allowance coming. Being relatively new to the
parenthood game, my memory kicked in immediately
and began calculating what it was that our allowance
might be paying for. Did we owe him for consuming
milk like a sieve so I can regularly go to the store for

more or was it for throwing up all over the bathroom
rug the day we returned from vacation? Or possibly we
were reimbursing him for leaving his jacket behind at
the restaurant booth and not noticing it until we got
home or for waking us during the night with nightmares.
My baser instincts were actually protesting the injustice
of a system which pays a person who has not yet
"cleaned up his act."

Eventually, after one struggles with the inequity of
allowance long enough, the realization sinks in that it is
no bargain. Allowance is, as all veteran parents know, a
payment for little or nothing. Put another way, it is a
payment on the future, a down payment which invests
on what the children are hoped to become. Such returns
may often seem to be minimal and slow in arriving. In
fact, they may not even be witnessed by the parents who
"paid the price for them."

My own inclination to barter with our children rather
than pay them may be related to my enrollment into the
seminary at the age of thirteen. There I encountered a
world where I was in some respects implicitly expected
to pole-vault adolescence and become a "paying adult."
We often come to expect of others what is expected of
us. So it is that the minister must make a choice in
dealing with the children of God. Are we to demand
payment for our gifts in the form of perfection or do we
"make allowance" for their messiness with an eye
toward their future Kingdom productivity?

Life With the Almighty
vs.
Life With "Mistakes"/"Accidents"

Ministers who feel that God is almighty form their ministry accordingly. They think that the answer to the most perplexing situations lies in divine providence and the rationale for the greatest human misery is found in God's will, incomprehensible though it may be. Armed with this realization, the minister is never at a loss for words. The fundamentalist preacher can demonstrate the cause/effect relationship between the sexual revolution and the outbreak of AIDS and so exhort people to the rewards of the straight and narrow. The minister who has experienced the "errors" of God's plan and divine "accidents," however, is not so quick on the draw with an explanation.

I like the conversation between the pastor and the seminarian in the film *Mass Appeal*. The youth is reluctant to say things to the bereaved because "everything I think of saying sounds so stupid." The priest prefers to offer condolences for he claims it makes people realize how inconsolable their grief is and it is just such an exalted position which gets most people through tragedies. So, for the pastor the anguish of death can be handled with words about a good life, a merciful death, or a heavenly reward: "This is one of the few areas where stupid is smart!" The seminarian, on the other hand, wonders, "Why do I have to say something? Can't I just listen?"

The believer in God Almighty, then, is spurred on to words of advice and explanation by that faith. One

schooled in divine limits, however, is not so quick to
take a mess lightly or simply explain it away. I
remember sitting in an airport with a couple who had
just lost a son to cancer. The father had the kind of faith
that was eager to get on with life. That was fine, but it
was not working for the mother, who was wrestling with
unresolved issues. As she strained to articulate her
dilemma, I simply said, "How do you feel about this?"
That direct question served to unlock a gate which
released her anger, fear, and doubts about God and life.
I just listened, amazed at how such a fundamental
question could pave the way to healing. She told me that
it was the first time she felt allowed to express these
darker feelings within her. Perhaps ministers in a messy
world will be much more likely to be hushed by people's
pain (just listen) and be willing to face it head on (there
is a serious problem here). Ministers in a messy world
are more prone to a pastoral co-responsibility which
makes the difference where God has "failed."

Life With the Cleanup Man
vs.
Life With the Guest

In the Gospel story of Martha and Mary, Martha's
priority was to clean house, while Mary chose to sit
down and be with her company. So it is that the minister
who images Jesus as one who came to clean things up
will be much more likely to straighten up the house first
and spend the leftover time visiting. In the same way,
the minister who identifies the mission of Jesus with
personal presence in a messy world feels comfortable

sitting down to communicate (experience communion) even when the house is not fully in order. As we deal with the coming of Jesus into our households, so will we be likely to set our expectations with regard to those who invite us to minister. We can either expect our hosts to straighten up their houses for our visit or we can encourage them to postpone the housework to be in our company.

When Jesus remains a cleanup man in our minds we hear and say statements like: "The Lord is really working in my life right now" or "God isn't finished with me yet." Such words suggest the image of a giant divine workshop with all of us as God's projects laying around on the benches and tables. As the Lord gets around to us we begin to take shape and become ready to go out and act as God's servants. In such a scenario we are relegated to a passive role until God fixes us or "puts on the finishing touches."

More recent pastoral language paints the image of a journey rather than of a divine workshop. In light of this development we might wish to reconsider the popular poem called "Footsteps." I would like to propose that becoming a minister in the image of Jesus as guest rather than as cleanup man may involve letting go of "footsteps" theology, as beautiful and helpful as it may be at certain times in our lives.

The words of "Footsteps" suggest that we walk with the Lord throughout our lives, except at those times when things are most difficult. It is at such points, as

Jesus proclaims in the poem, that the Lord carries us. For the minister in a messy world, called to embody divine love for the suffering, two questions arise:

1. Is the image of being carried an accurate portrayal of the experience of struggle in life?

2. Is it our primary responsibility as ministers to carry people through their crises?

We know when we are being carried because we feel safe and rested. Why then, at the end of the poem, does the Lord have to explain the significance of the single set of prints? It is precisely because the person did not feel carried but, true to experience, knew the struggle of going on with the journey. A much more accurate portrait of Jesus' presence to us is painted in Luke's account of the walk to Emmaus. Two disciples travel a road of bewilderment until the Lord joins them on the journey and makes all the difference: "Was it not necessary for the Messiah to suffer these things and then to enter his glory?" It is the act of carrying on with the journey rather than waiting to be carried that results in the revelation of divine presence: "Were not our hearts burning within us as he spoke to us on the road and explained the Scriptures to us?" and "They knew him in the breaking of the bread."

Jesus himself, while preparing in the desert for public ministry, experiences the temptation to abandon the journey for the comfort of a divine carrier. Satan bids Jesus to jump down from the temple so that: "God will bid the angels to take care of you; with their hands they will support you that you may never stumble on a stone" (Matt 4/6). Jesus does not carry us, then, but remains our guest. Resisting the temptation to prevent human stumbling by carrying us, the Lord bids us on as companions even when we stumble. He is our bread and company for the journey. So it is that we minister to one another, not by carrying each other around, but by accompanying one another and being food for one another in those times when life is most challenging and the journey is most tiresome. Ministry in the image of Jesus the guest involves first being at home with our hosts and then being present to them as they walk the road to Eucharist.

Life With the Doctor
vs.
Life With Patients (Patience)

When the church views herself as called to sustain the work that Jesus did in mending a broken world, the result can be a decision to put Jesus "on call" as attending physician. This move relegates the role of minister to a kind of spiritual ambulance, transporting patients to the hospital of the church where the divine physician can operate. In the fundamentalist view this operation is accomplished in the moment of being "born again," accepting Jesus as a personal savior or doctor. The underlying presupposition here is that the world which Jesus "fixed" has once again been tarnished, like a body reinfected with a virus. Only the sterile environment of the church, the spiritual hospital, can restore immunity and health, can allow rebirth in the spirit.

I recall a heartbreaking and yet, I must admit, very funny moment in the minor film entitled *Heartland.* In this scene the wife of a rugged Wyoming rancher is going into labor in the midst of winter. The husband believes that his duty is to fetch the doctor miles away, despite the raging blizzard outside. The man leaves his wife to brave the storm. Finally, after several days the cabin door blows open and the swirling snow ushers in the rancher. He shuts the door as a closeup reveals his face red with cold and his beard matted with ice and snow. His epic journey now complete, the rancher can only utter in straightforward exasperation: "He wasn't home." Slowly he looks closer at the bed and realizes that the baby has been born in his absence.

This tragic/comic scene clearly delineates a choice before the church. If our mission is to play nurse to the healing of Jesus then we must opt for responding to life situations (labor pains) by going for the doctor or getting people into the sterile confines of the hospital (church). As we continue to do this, however, we will be faced with the reality of many births in our absence. For life is born and dies with or without us. Our task is to be present in an image of the Lord as midwife. The life we cherish may be born and preserved much more effectively through our willingness to abandon the search for the doctor, who may not be home "out there." Instead we might choose to be present with patients/patience in the Lord who "stays home" as "Emmanuel."

Life Where Prayer Works
vs.
Life Where Pray-ers Work

Those ministers who live by the faith which proclaims that prayer changes things (prayer works) can always find an answer for failure that doesn't involve people changing things (pray-ers working). Answers are the hallmark of faith in the prayer that works. I remember the TV evangelist who was going through the bible showing how every Scriptural prayer was answered. When he got to one that didn't seem to fit that category he claimed that the angel bearing the answer arrived late.

While faith in the prayer that works is characterized by answers, the faith of a pray-er that works is identified by questions. In fact, it is the very involvement of such a person in the thick of the battle which gives rise to doubts and inquiries which form an integral part of his/her prayer life. It is this searching which gradually changes the person rather than changing things, making the minister more in touch with and responsive to human misery and need.

There is a saying which warns: "Be careful what you pray for; you just might get it." There is great truth here for the minister of prayer. The reason that we often get what we pray for lies in the dynamics of prayer reviewed earlier. Our prayer does not change God; prayer

changes us. Prayer does not activate God; it sends us
into action. So it is that our petitions do not talk God
into unplanned actions, but they dispose our hearts to
act: "Wherever your treasure is, there your heart will
be." The more we pray for something, the more likely
we are to obtain it because we become more convinced
of its value and our personal resources become more
directed toward its possession. When we pray "Thy will
be done" in the "Our Father," we are not speaking so
as to allow God to go ahead with divine plans, but to
remind and convince ourselves that God's will is the
best course for the world and rededicate our lives to its
accomplishment. Ministers in a messy world are called
to be careful what people pray for because such prayer
works in the sense that it gets pray-ers working on the
affectionate object of their prayer.

Signing the Order
vs.
Playing in the Mud

Liturgy is our public and official prayer. The world of
liturgy speaks volumes about our faith in God, Jesus,
the world, prayer, and the church, even as it writes new
pages each time it is celebrated. So it is that the
liturgical minister patterns the liturgy after the faith of
the church. If that faith tends toward the neatness of
Eden, the perfection of God, the repair work of the
Savior (reparation), the maintenance of the church, and
the prayer that works, it will be reflected in the liturgy.
If such faith accepts the originality of sin, the "errors"

of God, the company of Jesus, the "patience" of the church, and the pray-ers who work, that too will shine forth in its rituals.

Recall the old and repeated wisdom: "Pray as if everything depends on God and act as if everything depends on you." This pithy characterization of prayer emphasizes a dualism between God and the individual. Put another way it might read: "We do all the work and God gets all the credit." Moreover, our puny human efforts are really worthless, but they are important as tokens so that God will come in and save the day. Our prayers are valuable in that they acknowledge who is really behind the good that happens. This is the kind of spiritual advice that inevitably leads to the passivity and magical thinking that came to characterize pre-Vatican II liturgy.

What fools are going to keep pouring their guts out in efforts to change things when they believe deep down that those efforts are only tokens? If prayer is the real answer, we can sit back and "say the magic words" and God will surely do the deeds that need doing. So it is that Catholics began to relax in their pews and settle into private prayer while the priest made Jesus appear. Communal action was not part of the deal.

The "new liturgy," more appropriate for ministry in a messy world, stresses the unity of human and divine responsibility. Participation has been named the primary goal of renewed worship, not in order to get people off their "third knees," but rather because we have realized that things simply do not change without the efforts of people. Prayer and action cannot be so neatly separated. The new liturgy signs that faith by translating many of its prayers into the form of actions and gestures. Human efforts cannot be written off as "mere symbols," but are an integral means by which divine life is communicated. So it is that baptismal water is poured rather than dripped, confirmation oil is smeared rather than dabbed, and communion bread is baked to look and taste like real food.

Lourdes, a place that we will visit more in detail in a later chapter, serves as an environment for a liturgy of the infirm, the broken, the messy. Strange as it seems, the common image of Lourdes as a place where people celebrate their faith in the power of God is only a half-truth. In reality, the "liturgy" of Lourdes is just as vital for its role in allowing people to ritualize God's limits, to come to terms with divine letdowns. These prisoners of divine "accidents" arrive eager to celebrate the Lord's gift of freedom, to "sign the order" of their release. More often than not, however, they end up learning how to celebrate God's intimate presence in their infirmity, to "play in the mud" of their messy existence with God. This is why we might refer to Lourdes as a playground for the liturgy of the broken.

The Crux of Ministry in a Messy World

As I conclude this overview, it will serve us well to underscore what lies at the heart of successful contemporary ministry. These points form the fulcrum upon which all other considerations rest. Ministry in a messy world lives or dies by these basics:

1. We have argued that "God is not almighty" in the sense that the Lord gives power away rather than keeping it. The task of the minister, then, is to accept such power, to take on divine "response-ability." We have claimed that God is not in control insofar as the Lord elects to put power in motion rather than using it statically to maintain the status quo. In this regard the minister is called to move with divine power rather than resisting it, to be a channel of divine life: "Make me a channel of your peace." Here we see why humans are not puppets or tokens in a pastoral game. Once people are appreciated as "power-full" rather than helpless in ministry (God is "power-less" without us), vital weight is lent to our endeavors.

2. We have preferred the terms "mistake" and "accident" to words like "will," "purpose," and "limit" when pointing to human experiences of a breakdown in the divine plan. This has been intentional for the sake of stressing the necessary pastoral agenda for life's tragedies. The common human response to good (God) will is acceptance, but the normal reaction to a mistake is correction. With regard to things that are done "on purpose," people usually go along if they agree and move along or away if they don't, but they attend or minister to something that is an accident. Finally, we learn to accept our limits, but we always strive to overcome or transcend our mistakes and accidents. So it

is that from a pastoral perspective the words we have chosen ("mistake," "accident") are better human motivators for ministry than their counterparts ("will," "purpose," and "limit"). Our God "writes in pencil" when authoring our stories so that those elected as ministers can act to "erase the mistakes" (not the events, but the brokenness) before people read the wrong ending into their stories: "All is lost!"; "God isn't here!"; etc.

3. The concept of luck has been lurking in the shadows of many of the paths we have explored so far. We now bring "luck" out of the darkness and into our pastoral schema for its value in illustrating the human role in balancing the random nature of blessings. Too often in history, dating back to early Hebrew notions of God's workings, the unfortunate were outcasts because they were seen as victims of intentional divine curses: "Whose sin caused him to be born blind?" (John 9/2). TV evangelists employ similar arguments to justify their riches as well as their passivity in the face of poverty. Jesus converted that notion by pointing to the random nature of divine blessings: "God makes the rain to fall on the just and the unjust alike!" (Matt. 5/45). Ministers who are most blest will take charge of changing the bad luck of the poor into divine blessing. We must share what we have according to the way God dreams it rather than sitting back and enjoying "the way God made it." Material things will always involve luck, but people are the blessings who can change things around for the poor through personal investment.

4. Lastly, we have chosen a particular emphasis for the term "personal God." We have said that God is not "my personal God," a belief which leads to narcissism and isolation, but that our Lord is personal in the sense that God prefers to work through persons. We might remember the story of the farmer who inherited a plot of land filled with rocks and tree stumps. For months he labored to make it suitable for a rich harvest. In the fall of his first successful crop a neighbor dropped by and remarked that God had certainly blessed his land. The farmer paused a moment and then replied: "Maybe so, but you should have seen this place when God was working it alone!" Human effort and divine effort are one through the Incarnation. Ministry in a messy world realizes that fact.

The Minister's Choice

The age-old problem of evil always surfaces the disturbing question of God's relationship to human suffering. Is God the cause, the allower, or the helpless observer of our pain? In the film *Sophie's Choice* Meryl Streep plays a Jewish mother ordered to embody this dilemma in a diabolical fashion. Her Nazi captors torture her by forcing her to choose which of her two children will be condemned to death in the camps and which will be spared. It is one of the most haunting scenes I have ever witnessed on film. Indeed, the mother never recovers from the cruel choice that fate and human evil impose on her; it destroys her spirit.

So it is that those who believe in the Spirit of God at work in the world may find it impossible to opt for a God who selects life's victims, choosing who is to be condemned and who is to survive. Once we see that a mother can never make such a choice without jeopardizing her soul, we realize that God, our Mother, would compromise the integrity of her Spirit by executing such decisions. The minister in a messy world soon concludes that our divine Mother does not select the victim and dispense the pain, but chooses the minister and bestows the gift. The Lord's power is much more directed toward a creative, healing response to pain than toward a manipulation of the suffering that is an integral part of God's and our world.

As we look at the task ahead of us, the mission of being the presence of God to people in the midst of their brokenness and desperation, we again recall the plight of the quadriplegic from *Whose Life Is It Anyway?* We seek to be more than pill pushers who calm their own or others' questions with tranquilizers. The following chapters will seek to outline some of the particular ways we might become more effective ministers in a messy world.

Items for Individual Reflection/Group Process

1. Discuss the story of the quadriplegic. If possible, view the entire film: *Whose Life Is It Anyway?* Have we tended to "sedate" the cries of the suffering because of the difficult questions they raise? What are the challenges of confronting such painful questions? What are the advantages or lessons? Is it possible to remain open to intense doubt and still witness strong faith? How?

2. Get in touch with the experience of receiving allowance as a child and/or giving it as an adult. How do the two differ? In what ways has our pastoral ministry failed to "make allowance" for the adolescence of the church out of faith in a possible or developing future? In what ways has it succeeded? As ministers, how do we decide how much "allowance" to give?

3. Do you tend toward a style of ministry that talks (consoles, reasons) or one that listens (is silenced)? What have been your successes and failures with each approach?

4. Does the "Footprints" poem inspire you to go on with the journey? Why or why not? Do you experience Jesus primarily as a carrier (Footprints) or as a companion (Emmaus)? Explain.

5. How is the church called to participate in the birth of new life? Do we call the doctor or learn to be present with patience? Identify examples of each approach in the ministry of the modern church. What are the dualistic elements in the tendency to "call the doctor"? In some respects have men's self-appointed duty of "going for the doctor" left women to endure the labor pains of birthing new life within the church? How?

6. When we pray, "Thy will be done," what are we asking for? Are we giving God the okay to proceed with the plan or is personal commitment part of the ordinary person's understanding of this

phrase? Are we "talking to ourselves" with this prayer? What pray-er work needs to be engaged if God's dream is to prevail on earth?

7. Have you developed an ability to celebrate the Lord's presence "in the mud" (like God's children at Lourdes do)? If not, how can such a capacity be acquired? What are some other examples of God's children "playing in the mud"?

8. The author chooses the words "mistake" and "accident" to refer to divine limits in order to underscore the integral role of human participation through ministry to correct mistakes and attend to accidents (rather than to accept limits). Is this acceptable to you? Are there other ways of making this point?

Activities for Pastoral Staffs/Ministries

1. Form an action plan for Christian AIDS education in your parish
   or community (Chicago already has a diocesan program in
   place). Address the fears and prejudices that are surfaced by
   such endeavors. How can they be effectively challenged? For
   those with a school child or an adult member with AIDS, this
   issue is more urgent. Might our fears regarding contact with
   AIDS, a disease which attacks our immune system, be related to
   our desire to remain immune, our reluctance to become
   vulnerable? How does this apply to the risk element in ministry?

2. Take the Myers Briggs test as a staff. Have a facilitator process
   the results with you with a view toward understanding the basic
   approach that each person takes to ministry. Note where there
   are conflicts, where there is complementarity, and how team
   ministry might be affected. Sample tensions are: "I" (centering)
   vs. "E" (outreach); "N" (hunch) vs. "S" (facts); "F" (heart) vs.
   "T" (head); and "P" (openness) vs. "J" (closure).

3. Discuss the implications of our "disposable world" and our
   "instant world" for ministry. The progress that allows us to enjoy
   disposable income and disposable diapers also burdens us with
   disposable spouses (divorce), disposable infants (aborted or
   found in trash cans), and a disposable environment (pollution). A
   society that values instant cameras, coffee, and breakfast also
   expects "instant grace" (cheap grace). How do these trends in
   society rear their heads in your parish or community? What
   measures can be taken to encourage people to "keep each other"
   rather than dispose of each other, and to "take time" for grace
   rather than seek instant grace?

4. Evaluate efforts in your parish or community toward vocation
   awareness. Find out to what extent adults and children still
   identify "vocation" with ordained, professed, or professional
   ministry. Are your own pastoral efforts still geared toward
   recruiting "religious vocations?" Draw up a new program that

will speak the need for "everyone to have a vocation." Also determine the role of women in that plan. Does our tendency to identify church leadership with the male image speak of our desire to continue fashioning ministry according to male qualities like logic and control as opposed to female gifts like intuition and openness?

5. Discuss historical figures who might be considered as divine "mistakes" or "accidents" according to the principles of this book: Hitler, the Elephant Man, John Gacy, etc. Consider what methods of "correction" might be employed that you would regard as Christian. The story of Helen Keller provides one heroic example. This issue raises questions about the use of violence, the effectiveness of penal institutions, capitol punishment, medical ethics, etc.

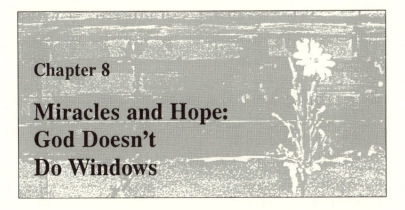

Chapter 8

Miracles and Hope: God Doesn't Do Windows

"He could work no miracles there because of their lack of faith."
— Mark 6/5-6

Recently, in one of those rare moments of candidness about life that usually occurs only after both parent and child have separated, "grown up," and "re-membered," my mother told a childhood story. The story was about one of her favorite aunts who lived next door to her family while she was growing up. Mom was so fond of this aunt that she often spent hours there after school visiting and helping out. In time she learned that she had to choose those visiting hours carefully, for during her stays the sickness and cruelty of her uncle became increasingly evident. My mother was the victim of her uncle's abuse on one occasion, and fear of repeated episodes often overshadowed the joy of the time spent with her aunt. Much more common and frightening, however, was the constant verbal, emotional, and physical abuse her aunt suffered at the hands of this man.

My mother told of how she would watch for the "safe times" and then hurry over to see her aunt. When it was time for her uncle to arrive she would slip out the back and return home. While her aunt never said much about the dark existence she knew with her husband, my mother had a sense of what she was escaping each time she left, as well as what her aunt could not escape. Her aunt had approached the church regarding the possibility of a divorce, but such things were simply not done then. For her, there was no way out of the horrible trap her life had become.

One day my mom went over for an after school visit, but no one answered the door. She considered going in, but thought better of it and returned home. Later that day there was a knock at the door, recalled through the haunting image of a broom handle rapping against the door frame. Her uncle had come over to inform them that he had just discovered his wife dead in the basement. She had hanged herself there earlier in the day. In the time that followed the tragedy my mother learned that the church had refused to give her aunt a Catholic burial.

Miracles and Reading the Signs of the Times

This may seem like a grim tale with which to begin a reflection on hope, but it is relevant for its power to demythologize the past. Frequently we carry with us a sense that the messiness of contemporary life is a recent development, that things were much brighter and happier "in the old days." The gift given by those who tell the truth about their historical experience is the revelation that much of the messiness of contemporary life is not new, but simply more apparent. In the good old days our faith and hope allowed us to participate in a well-intentioned coverup of what life was really like. In these times of storytelling and reflectivity, however, there is simply too much evidence to bring off such an enterprise successfully.

What shape, then, is a ministry of hope to assume? What in our past can we draw hope from? What in the present can we hope in? What in our future are we to hope for? What is false hope or illusion and how are we to separate it from authentic faith in obscure or unseen spiritual reality? These are some of the questions which our ministry for a messy world must answer in order to determine what sort of hope we offer as followers of Jesus.

We grew up in an age of miracles. People flocked to Marian devotions to seek or report divine favors. "Poor souls" could be rescued from purgatory or guaranteed heaven by uttering the right prayers at the right time. Catholic Eucharist wasn't limited to the figurative presence of mere symbols, but effected "real presence" through the miracle of physical transubstantiation. The Bible was eagerly read to provide historical accounts of literal wonders (the import of less literal storytelling truths had somehow gotten lost along the way). And what Christian youth did not sometimes beg for an ambitious miracle in the form of a new bike for Christmas from poor parents, the sudden recovery of a terminal grandparent, or the "disappearance" of the neighborhood bully?

The starting point for a ministry of hope in a messy world is the truth that such an "age of miracles" is now past or, in view of my mother's story, was never truly with us. We may need to admit to ourselves and to others that there are few miracles of the kind we were once taught to believe in and desire. In the movie *Oh God!* George Burns, as God, says it this way: "I don't do miracles; they're too flashy and they upset the natural balance. Oh, once in a while, just to keep my hand in. The last miracle I did was the '69 Mets." Now, we don't want to base our theology on Hollywood, but there is a piece of truth here to be examined.

The experience of people, when it is honestly reflected upon, confirms our suspicion that the miracles of our youth are no more to be counted on as the basis for our hope. To be more precise, we are in an age when we must redefine the miraculous in order to bring it into line with human experience. We must reexamine what we have called "a miracle" in the past to see if we were perhaps mistaken or misguided in our zeal to sweep our mess under a miraculous carpet rather than enter and transform it.

Much of the miraculous is a matter of vision. Two people observe the same event, one sees a glorious sign while another views it as blind fate. A child is walking across the street as a car veers out of control. A passerby rushes out just in time to push the little girl out of the way. The believer in miracles sees the hand of God at work in this event; the atheist names this "dumb luck" and remains unmoved. More will be said later about the relationship of vision to miracles. For now, though, we will address a more direct question: If we are to maintain that divine power is active in the world, working wonders that speak God's marvelous presence, how might such faith in the miraculous be rearticulated so as to be compatible with the ambiguity of human experience?

In order to answer this question it is helpful to do a case study of similar crisis situations. These reflections do raise certain difficulties and inconsistencies. If answers to crises are truly miraculous, why are they not more common; that is, why do tragedies occur at all if God has the power to intervene with a miracle to prevent them? Another problem is the inequitable distribution of miracles. If God is the author of miracles, why are they so inefficiently managed? If the Lord miraculously protects us, what do we make of the "coincidence" that the rich are better shielded than the poor? If surviving an auto accident is a miracle, why does the drunk driver walk away while the innocent mother of three children is killed? How does a good God determine which people and situations are worthy of miraculous intervention?

Miracles and Luck

The luck dimension of blessings cited earlier has particular relevance when discussing miracles. Sufficient study of passages from the human storybook leads us to sobering conclusions which may have to be faced if our ministry of hope is to be successful. In time, life teaches us that what we have named "miraculous" is often a matter of good luck, just as much that we have assigned to "the wrath of God" or God's punishment is more properly called "bad luck." Any other hypothesis leads us to hope in an uncaring or inefficient God who dispenses miraculous blessings arbitrarily with no regard for the concrete circumstances of human lives. If we are to be effective ministers of hope amid life's messiness, we might begin our training by renaming many of our miracles as good luck, for such a naming process holds considerable implications for the shape of pastoral care.

The intention here is not to assign life's wonders to some nameless and impersonal cosmic force ("I'm not gas!" George Burns protests in *Oh God!*), but to recall my earlier point that the Creator does not control the application of these blessings. Consequently, miracles are not lucky in the general or cosmic sense that reduces their very existence to chance. Miracles are lucky, however, in the specific or earthy sense that recognizes a random nature to their occurrence that is subject to various factors. Among these circumstances are power, race, geography, time, and sin. Once we accept this we can adopt healthier, more responsible reasons for why Americans witness more "miracles" than Third World nations (life, health, affluence, freedom).

The most vital consequence of calling miracles "luck" is evident: Amid a scarcity of signs from above, we become God's signs. As people cease to await wonders from the sky, they can begin to look to us to be miracles for them and even come to find miracles in themselves and others. The letting go of our past definition of the miraculous is not an exercise in despair, but the opening of a door to new pathways of hope, new sources of transforming power. It is in this context that the redefinition of the miraculous can be worded thus: A miracle is a revelation of divine power and presence through "ordinary" human existence. Put in another way, it is the power to open our eyes to wonders that are already here and put them to work toward the dawning of the Kingdom of God.

Lourdes: Melting Pot of Miraculous Faith

The willingness to let go of comfortable models of the miraculous is not easily acquired. The passive spirituality that tempts us to "wait for God to do it" is still deep in our pre-Vatican II bones, along with the dualistic theology which views human and divine efforts as separate or opposed. Yet, if we are to be effective ministers of hope, this task is vital. In the end, we must teach people what they may realistically hope for from God and from humanity. As there are problems with defining the miraculous in terms of what happens to people, perhaps we must shift our focus to an understanding of miracles in terms of what happens in people. A recent CBS "60 Minutes" report on Lourdes provides three profiles which may assist us in this task. Each of these stories tells of a search for one kind of miracle and the discovery of another. These believers prayed to have their lives changed and found that they were changed by life.

Mary Lou brought her paralyzed husband, Jim, to Lourdes in search of a miracle cure. Each time her husband was lowered into the water they shared the hope that he might walk out on his own power. Yet, after five visits to the shrine, this has still not happened. Instead, Jim employs a laborious sign language to describe the "alternate miracle" that has occurred: "My eyes were opened." The exact nature of this couple's blindness is unclear, but the reality of their new vision is unmistakable. For those who witness their fidelity and perseverance, this conversion becomes in itself a miracle of hope. We witness not a physical sign, but wonders of the heart.

Beth arrived at Lourdes with a broken heart after the sudden death of her 36-year-old husband. She came in search of healing, convinced that the salve for her wound was an answer to the question "Why?": "I could either say, 'God, how could you do this to me?' or I could say, 'There's a reason and I have to accept it.'" Yet, the real miracle of that pilgrimage was the metanoia born of her prayer: "I'm praying to stop asking why." In uttering that prayer she already had an initial glimpse of the miracle she sought. By letting go of her question Beth had taken the first step toward healing, a step that was foremost a journey of faith.

Finally, there was Maggie, a young girl paralyzed at birth from cerebral palsy. Her parents longed for a miracle cure, but soon came to marvel at the miraculous spirit of their daughter. Maggie is a miracle of compassion. Instead of indulging in self pity, her concerns are focused upon others. When the journalist asks what she prays for when she enters the baths, she explains that she prays for her dad's back to get straighter. Maggie's disease has taught her compassion. She sees the pain of others and suffers with them. What greater miracle is there in life?

People may always flock to churches where icons shed tears, eager to ritualize their faith in a God of miracles. There is nothing terribly wrong with such things in themselves, for there is always a transcendent element to God's action to be accounted for. Yet, searching for such signs takes energy, and one wonders whether crying icons deserve as much of our spiritual resources as crying humanity. Do not too many earthy miracles wait for our attention to spend ourselves in the quest for heavenly ones? How can we be so preoccupied with these "miracles from the sky" that we overlook countless "miracles of the earth?" In the same way, I suppose, that the people missed the birth of the Savior in a stable while they were looking for a powerful warrior from on high. In any case, those who are willing to lower their gazes to view the marvels of Emmanuel's miraculous presence will soon find that their dealings with one another are called to conversion.

There are real consequences to altering our perspective of the miraculous to be a more wholistic, Incarnational one. Here are six ways of ministering toward hope in the mess that will, hopefully, allow more frequent and equitable miracles to be realized among us.

1. Don't Expect Too Many Miracles

The realization that divine miracles are not always at the disposal of the faithful requires that we deal with life and people carefully and compassionately. One obvious example is the church's ban on artificial birth control. Our adherence to the teaching of natural law is based upon the belief that an openness to creation will always be reciprocated with the power to respond to its demands. This is related to the "God will only send you what you can handle" myth cited earlier. Such faith has frequently resulted in large families visited with poverty, child abuse, and disintegration.

Life, God's creation, does weigh some people down with intolerable burdens. The consequences of asking people to go to the well of human generosity and endurance far too often may bring us to accept "miracles" like the pill. Perhaps if fewer miracles had been expected of my mother's aunt, and more real alternatives had been provided, she could have recognized the "miracle" in such ministry and not resorted to the dead end of suicide, the ultimate loss of hope.

2. See People as Miracles

The complementary virtue to not expecting unrealistic things is the personal affirmation that allows us to expect great things from one another. This begins with our own ecclesial faith in the manifestation of the Spirit by the human heart. How many papal messages in recent years have exuded this faith in a humanity made in God's image? How many, instead, have harped upon our depravity and failures, and our constant need for being policed? Part of the problem may be the press, which tends to accentuate the negative. If this is so, we must double our efforts to get the positive message through. Perhaps, though, we do need to test the depth of our belief in the Incarnation, in the power of the followers of Jesus to perform the same wonders he did.

One such test might involve a review of church processes for canonization. This system, requiring the documentation of three miracles as a criterion for sainthood, is a sign of the literal-minded reluctance with which we recognize people as miraculous, saintly. Contrast this with our relatively liberal application of the word "sinner" and the comparative ease with which a person can be numbered in that category. Possibly when we are less stingy in recognizing and naming the saintliness in people, we will find ourselves more disposed to seeing people as miraculous. With such a vision, rather than straining to find three miracles in a life, we may find ourselves hard pressed to limit the number of miracles we discover in people's lives.

3. Steward a Miraculous World

Disasters and ominous threats to creation are often the result of human interference in the naturally miraculous workings of the cosmos. Miracles like the regeneration of topsoil, the natural rhythms of seasons, and the production of oxygen are daily being threatened, not by divine failure, but by human irresponsibility. As we exploit the land with chemicals, disrupt weather patterns with pollution and nuclear arms tests, and lay waste to rain forests, we face a critical shortage of nature's innate miracles.

Just as a scarcity of natural signs and wonders is often the price of our sins against nature, so is a dearth of miracles of healing the consequence of our sins against the body. Alcohol and drug abuse, radiation, smoking, stress, etc. wreak havoc on natural bodily functions that are truly biological miracles. The growing statistics of cancer, birth defects, heart disease, and mental illness cannot be blamed on God alone, but must also be laid at the doorstep of our assault on the body's God-given healing powers. A commitment on our part to move away from the dualism of Fall/Redemption theology to the miracle affirming faith of Creation theology will pave the way for a renewed celebration of such miracles which will allow people enough hope to better steward these gifts.

4. Make Allowances for Mistakes

One of the most disturbing trends in the world today is our shrinking capacity to allow people to make mistakes, to be imperfect. Perfection is demanded in work and play, mind and body. Possibly one of the most significant barometers of this movement is the proliferation of malpractice suits against doctors and hospitals. While admitting the human potential for negligence, we might reflect upon the origin and implications of our war on doctors. Perhaps it is a response to the letdown we experienced after all the hype about the miracles of modern medicine. Maybe we are not able to cope with the failure of our physicians to rescue us from disability and death at the hands of disease. Possibly our anger at the limited number of medical miracles is played out in courtrooms where money becomes the panacea for our woes. We might also speculate as to whether these attacks on our doctors is not a transference of our anger toward God for not providing the miracles we were taught to expect from youth.

Just as we eventually come to terms with the "mistakes" of God, learning to forgive the Lord just as God has first forgiven us, so must we accept the very real limitations of God's people. Ministers may need to begin their work with a keen sense of the fragility of their people. People, in turn, may facilitate the effectiveness of their ministers by adjusting their personal expectations of such pastoral care. In the end, we do not offer hope to one another by exacting perfection at a great price, but by being as mutually accepting and healing of our human limitations as is the Lord.

5. Let the Search Continue

In a world where miracles are desperately needed but in radically short supply, no undertaking is more vital to the success of a ministry of hope than that of searching out new avenues of divine power. Within the context of the church we call those searchers "theologians." Theologians make modern miracles possible by reconciling human activity with our images of God. This is essential because their "scouting" legitimizes worldly miracles while aiding us in letting go of false promises of "signs from above." In their eyes we find a synthesis which shuns dualism in favor of Incarnational reciprocity. Theologians who question the indissolubility of marriage, moreover, allow a battered wife to stop waiting for a "sign from above" and instead search within for the miraculous courage to get help, to separate or divorce. A review of mandatory celibacy opens options beyond cold showers and "Hail Marys" to clergy debilitated by loneliness. Tendencies toward the silencing of dissenting or searching theologians does not bode well for the future of this enterprise.

6. Go Tell It on a Mountain

The task of evangelization is vital to the future of hope in the church. The more we spread the Good News, the more "other Christs" will be operative in the world, the less we will have to rely on luck for God's love to touch humankind. It is here that we return to the atheist and the believer witnessing the car accident. The atheist is right that there is an element of luck in the girl being pulled away from the onrushing car by a passerby. We can well imagine the girl commenting: "Lucky for me you came along." Yet, this does not take God out of the picture. It is the Spirit of God, not luck, which moves a casual observer to jump out and risk his life for another. As the experience of Spirit becomes more widespread, the chances that such an event will be mere luck decrease and the odds that it will be a "miracle," a manifestation of God's Incarnational presence, increase. The rescued girl may in turn take a personal risk for another later in life. One of our missions as ministers of hope is to up the odds for miracles by touching as many as possible with God. Ministers are like magnifying glasses which direct divine life onto needy individuals so that God's blessings do not remain random or unfocused.

Miracles: Dreams or Fantasies?

In the end, no task is more central to the formation of our ministry of hope than the purification of our dreams and imaginations. The importance of dreams and imagination is rather well recognized in the church today. However, we also know that our visions and fantasies can work toward escapism rather than engagement. The minister of hope in a messy world, aware of the human condition, will allow for a healthy amount of escape fantasy, but ultimately seeks to release the power of transformation which such imagining holds in store. The minister of hope is called

to allow her own and others' dreams and imaginations
to be purified and empowered as agents of personal,
ecclesial, and global transformation.

Such a miracle happens through the giving over of
oneself to those encounters which teach us to be
human, to dream creatively. The fruits of such a process
are visions and ideals which strike a crucial balance
between bleak realism and naive fantasy. The
experiences which take us through this purifying process
will leave us more active and increasingly human and
alive. As our dreams mature we will leave the old ones
behind and go on to more challenging ones. The
balance between blissful fantasies which are destructive
in their passive unrealism and creative dreams which
lead us to personal engagement is a hard one to achieve.
As ministers of hope in a messy reality, which dreams
are we to discourage and which are we to develop? A
brief look at two films may provide guidelines for this
discernment process.

The first film is Woody Allen's *The Purple Rose of
Cairo*. It tells the story of a woman who escapes a cruel
and loveless home life by going to the cinema. At the
movies she enters the romantic fantasies which her hard
personal life lacks. Soon, much to her surprise, one of
the characters she loves from afar walks off the screen
and into her life. She falls in love with this character and
claims the happiness she has so long sought: "He's
fictional, but you can't have everything!" This joy,
however, is not to go unchallenged. Soon the real life
actor who portrays the film character arrives to
convince her to allow him back into the movie. The

heroine is faced with a most difficult choice: "Do I re-enter the real world or live out my days with a fantasy?" She chooses the real world and runs off to meet the actor who has promised to take her back to Hollywood. When she arrives at their meeting place she is told that he has left without her. The final scene of the film shows her back in the cinema escaping into another movie.

This is a brilliant portrayal of the dilemma we face as dreamers and ministers of hope. We must choose between the security of comforting fantasyland and the perils of real life encounters. Woody Allen does not make it easy on us by opting to have the heroine's one leap toward creative engagement end in tragedy. Yet, the saddest part of the film is not this setback, but the result. Her engagement with reality does not change her. She will not allow her fantasy to be purified by life. Instead she compromises her dream and remains with her cruel husband even as she returns to the theatre for escape. Here is an example of a fantasy that leads to death, passivity, and withdrawal, as well as a statement that the risk of engagement does not protect us from failure and disappointment.

The second example, a story of lifegiving fantasy, is the film *Breaking Away*. Here, too, we have someone who lives out a dream. In order to escape the social stigma of being a "cutter" (stone cutter) an Indiana youth assumes the identity of an Italian bicycle racer. He changes his name, listens to opera, speaks Italian around the house, and serenades the girl of his dreams. He trains hard to be a bicycle racing champion in the image of the Italian racing team he idolizes. His antics infuriate his father who is always trying to get him to "face reality" according to his own cynical outlook: "No, I don't feel lucky to be alive; I feel lucky I'm not dead. There's a difference."

As in *Purple Rose*, the dream is shattered by the intrusion of reality. The Italian racers he idolizes turn out to be cruel cheats and he succumbs to his father's plea that he "see life as it is!": "Everyone cheats; I just didn't know." The difference here is not in the conflict, but in the response to the conflict. For while the youth is forced to drop the unreal portion of his fantasy (I am not a cutter), the creative part of it remains (cutters are more than they seem). Faced with the escapist part of his dream, he is able to rescue the portion that is engaging and transforming. By training for and winning the bicycle race at the end of the film, he energizes and redeems the lives of his friends and family, especially his relationship with his father.

So it is that our dreams may either immobilize us or creatively engage us in the human enterprise. It is the ministry of hope in a messy world to inspire people to stay with their creative dreams even in the face of life's harsh realities. It is this minister of hope who will see such visions and offer them as blueprints for transforming the world into a miracle in Christ.

The Hebrew Vision of Miracles

This brings us back to the issue of vision raised earlier. Because of our Greek/western roots, with their emphasis on the literal and pragmatic, these pages can be seen as a denial of our Judeo-Christian heritage of faith in a God who works great signs and wonders in our midst. Yet, in reality, these ideas are quite compatible with our image of a Yahweh-God made incarnate in Jesus. The Hebrew faith that forms the basis for Christianity is born of a vision which sees reality as permeated with the power and presence of the Lord. This faith is much more concerned with impression than appearance (how an event strikes a people more than its physical description) and with symbolism than instrumentalism (what an event means for a people rather than what it does for them). Whether experiencing exile or exodus, sunrise or sunset, feast or famine, the people of Israel viewed such events as signs of the action of the Lord in their lives. This faith vision allowed them to see God's presence in the "ordinary," to realize that there is no such thing as ordinary, with a conviction unsurpassed in the history of world religions.

It is such faith that allows us to proclaim the presence of God in our midst without having to resort to a denial of human limits. It is the lack of such vision that limits the Lord's power: "He could work no miracles there because of their lack of faith." The word "religion" does not exist in the Hebrew vocabulary, since such a word would hint of a distinction between God-experience and human experience. In the same way, it is quite possible to delete the word "miracle" from the Jewish language, if by such a term we mean an experience of the power and presence of the Lord as distinct from or over/above everyday life.

To put it another way, according to the Hebrew vision, all of creation is miraculous. So, whether the exodus was accomplished through a miracle (God intervening to part the mighty waters of the Red Sea to allow the chosen people to escape) or a "miracle" (the Lord leading the people through the windswept shallows of the Sea of Reeds) is irrelevant. Whatever occured, we can be sure that in the vision of Hebrew faith there was found great reason to rejoice and hope in a God who was ever present and active in bringing them forth to a new and promised land of freedom. These eyes of faith which viewed all of reality as holy, especially humanity, gave rise to an "earthy" perception of miracles that is well defined in the following story:

My sister almost died some months ago. For weeks she and her roommate experienced nausea, disorientation, and drowsiness, but passed it off as the flu. One night Pat awoke in the midst of a nightmare and knew that something was terribly wrong. She was so weak that she had to roll off the bed, crawl downstairs, and alert her roommate who had fallen asleep in a chair: "We've got to get out of here!" A day in the hospital brought recovery, but no explanation for their condition. Upon arriving home, the symptoms recurred with a vengeance. This time the doctor caught on. He had them open the windows and kept Pat on the phone until the ambulance arrived. The hospital's diagnosis confirmed his suspicions. They were suffering from carbon monoxide poisoning. Blood tests revealed a forty-five count of this toxin in their systems. The fatal level is sixty.

My mother, shaken as she was, proclaimed her daughter's survival a miracle. While inclined to agree, I wondered what sort of miracle it was and who had performed it. A news story in Chicago earlier that week reported a family who had fallen asleep in similar circumstances. None of them woke up. Why had my sister survived under the same conditions for weeks? Part of the reason was luck: Pat lived in a drafty house. Part of it was mystery: the nightmare that had awaken her. Yet, when I asked Pat, she gave a simple, but significant explanation. While homebound with the "flu," she had received constant phone calls from co-workers, friends, and family. Time after time, it turns out, these calls saved her life by awakening her from a deadly sleep.

Maybe this is the definition of a miracle for our times. We live in an age when all of us are dying from the many poisons in our spiritual and physical environments. Yet, society tends to normalize these ills and deaden us to their harmful impact, so that many "die in their sleep." It is only our constant caring for each other, our calling each other forth, which wakes us up and keeps us truly alive. Perhaps it is in such simple human acts that, amid our pain and doubt, there may be hope for us yet!

Items for Individual Reflection/Group Process

1. State your "working definition" of a miracle. How has your definition changed over the years? What experiences have brought about that change? How readily have you let go of former notions of the miraculous? Have you never felt the need to refashion your belief in miracles? Why not?

2. What might the statement "the age of miracles is past" mean for today's world and for today's minister? Is the Cecil B. DeMille vision of miracles gone forever? Why or why not?

3. Can some miracles be called "luck," as the author suggests, or is this a lack of faith? What is the writer trying to get at by this claim? What are the advantages and liabilities of using such a term?

4. Does it feel like a letdown to you to describe miracles in less literal, more "ordinary" ways? Why or why not?

5. What is your reaction to the phrase: "We are now the miracles."? Do you experience people as miraculous? How? As our notion of the miraculous is "incorporated," what are its implications for ministry?

6. Are you able to affirm your faith on the basis of "ordinary" miracles, or do you feel it is vital that God intervene in the natural order with powerful signs of divine presence? What does your preference say about God?; about people?

7. Is there a place for weeping statues and prophetic apparitions in the life of the church? What is it? Do such things build up a creative, participatory ministry, or do they lead to magical thinking and passivity?

8. If God were a Lord of miracles, why would he choose to come to us on manger and cross? How is an "extraordinary" model of the miraculous reconciled with the "ordinary" advents of God?

9. Would you travel to Lourdes, Fatima, or Medjugorje if you "needed a miracle"? What would you be looking for? What would you hope to happen? What pastoral sense are we to make of the Lord's angry reaction toward those who demanded a miracle: "How evil and godless are the people of this day! You ask me for a miracle? No!" (Matt 12/39)? What is Jesus criticizing?

Activities for Pastoral Staffs/Ministries

1. Share with each other some of the miracles that have occured in the parish or community. Reflect upon these wonders in terms of what happened objectively (out there) and subjectively (in people). What does this say about the shape of hope in the community?

2. A follow-up to #1 above would be a brainstorm session on the miracles that are needed in the parish or community. Again, if these miracles are to take place, what needs to happen objectively (out there) and what needs to happen subjectively (in people)? How can the group facilitate this occurence?

3. Look at the support structures within the pastoral team and in the community. How are people supported (given hope)? Does the group or parish tend toward divine intervention ("I'll pray for you!" "God bless you!"), or is there a "hands on" style that real-izes the miracle of human intervention ("What can I do for you?")? Ask the members of the group to share the extent to which they feel supported and what concrete measures might help them experience needed support.

4. Assess the extent to which traditional faith elements in the parish either support or inhibit mature community ministry, ie. the human participation necessary for miracles to occur. Perhaps some work could be done with them in a faith sharing context. The "60 minutes" report might be useful (transcripts are available from CBS) or any other resource that breaks open faith and paves the way for reflection on alternative theological models for understanding apparitions and miracles.

5. Discuss the group's expectations of one another and of the community at large. How are those expectations defined, expressed, and experienced by the people involved? How do we draw the best, the miracles, from one another? Apply positive and negative strategies for success from the business world. The

book *In Search of Excellence* by Tom Peters and Robert
Waterman is a fine resource. The approach of that book might be
contrasted with the image of boot camp, where "spit and polish"
is the methodology for achievement and excellence: "Be all that
you can be, find your future in the army."

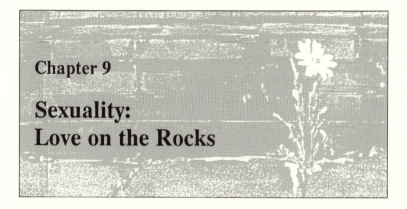

Chapter 9

Sexuality:
Love on the Rocks

"Losing love is like a window in your heart;
Everybody sees you're blown apart.
Everybody feels the wind blow."
— Paul Simon: "Graceland"

It was Christmas and I was ten years old. I waited
upstairs as long as I could, though I was bursting to get
out of bed and descend to the fantasyland that I knew
awaited me around the tree in the living room. I don't
recall why my brothers and sister were not stirring, but I
do know that I will never forget that Christmas. I gave in
to my excitement and hurried downstairs in wonder.
When I reached the foot of the staircase, I stared into
the kitchen in disbelief and confusion. "Today can't be

Christmas," I thought, for my mother was standing by the sink crying. She said that her father had died during the night.

Grandpa had recently been released from the hospital and was recovering at our house over the holidays. He had been doing fine until he made the mistake of chancing the cold December air to fetch the newspaper. He had caught pneumonia. Grandpa would not be spending Christmas with us and we would not be spending Christmas in the usual way. Something of the fantasy died in me that year. Jesus normally came for me by way of stockings and toys, but from then on I began to look for him in other "wrappings."

Love is in the Air (the Wind)

The title of this chapter is intended to incorporate the many ways our "love boats," our fantasies of love, capsize on the rocks of reality. We dream of staying in love or keeping love, but the truth of life is that we inevitably "fall out of love" or lose love. Our many loves may escape this fate for a while, but eventually we all face a day when we must say good-bye to persons or dreams we hold dear (grandfathers, Christmas ideals). Yet, as Paul Simon reflects, losing these loves opens windows in our hearts. It is clear that we are shattered by such losses (blown apart), but there is also evidence of the potential power of the Spirit for new life and purpose (everybody feels the wind blow). This chapter is about admitting the losses, letting go of unreal fantasies, and capturing the wind in our sails that blows the promise of the Spirit from the death of love's fantasies.

Ministers of love in a messy world are called to be the glue that holds people together in those times of being "blown apart" and the arrow that points them in the new direction the Spirit's wind is blowing. If we are to succeed at this, we must submit our love to the same purifying process. Ministry too is subject to unreal fantasies about God's love and how it is preserved. Ministers strive to "stay in love" with God (keep divine love), but their ministry is truly transformed by the Spirit when it is blown apart by "losing God's love" as they had fantasized about it. Our time will be well spent if we examine four of our historical and ongoing fantasies about divine love. What is there in these fantasies that we might be called to release? What is it about love that, if discovered and embraced, might bring new life to the world?

Fantasy 1: Love Without Sex

Every spring we knew it was coming. No year in the seminary would be complete without it. We seminarians could not be abandoned to the world for the summer without our annual "girl talk." This, of course, was not a talk about girls, but a lecture about avoiding girls. Our vocation to love people, the unspoken logic assumed, could only be safeguarded by staying clear of the perils of femininity, by sublimating sexual energy into more noble and Godly tasks. Thus, women were implicitly deleted from the ranks of the people we were preparing to love. So it was that while working my first summer job I resisted a mutual attraction with a waitress by valiantly taking refuge in my priestly destiny. That this noble purity was most conducive to my development as a whole ministerial person is questionable. In fact, others would pay a price for my resultant sexual immaturity later on.

The fantasy, of course, is that love is kept divine or Godly when it is spiritual and pure. The nightmare is that love sinks to the secular or tainted when it is sexual and bodily. How sad it is to realize that our faith in the Virgin birth has yielded a horrible "mis-conception" that God would never stoop to come into the world via the sex act, that sex cannot conceive of the Lord. Celibacy, then, becomes the vehicle for fulfilling a fantasy of perfect divine love. The theology which views celibate love as a positive charism for achieving a special grace is overshadowed by this fantasy which creates a spiritual vacuum. It is significant that in the minds of many Christians the opposite of "sexual" is "celibate," implying that celibate persons sacrifice sexuality. The truth that celibate and conjugal love are manifestations of different facets of the same divine love is only recently being rescued and rearticulated in Christian theology.

In order to let go of such a negative view of both celibacy and sex, a key question which must be addressed is whether the introduction of sex does send the love relationship spinning out of control and away from the divine sphere of things. In other words, is sex a threat to the transmission of divine love? Must the instruments of divine/spiritual love be shielded from the dangers of human/bodily love? Must repression and isolation be the means by which religious vocations are prevented from being "lost"? My seminary training in the sixties was based on affirmative answers to those questions. Do the eighties offer us any alternatives?

Experience confirms the potentially explosive power of sex, a threat which no amount of warning or protection will forestall. I was given a shield to guard my priestly destiny that worked for a time, for I resisted the Woolworth waitress, but it could not and would not endure. When I was in college I met a woman while attending a workshop in the East. There was an attraction there that drew us together as the week progressed. By week's end we spoke of possibilities, such as a choice to leave the seminary, that would allow us to further unfold our relationship. After parting we corresponded for weeks. There was unfocused longing and considerable struggle in those letters, but they gradually tapered off as our basic life values at the time reasserted themselves, something like the default settings on a computer.

A few years later the destructive potential of sex reared its head again while I was engaged to a young woman (recall the wedding hat story). The wonder of our love was born of romantic fantasy: "I feel like I'm in a musical," she had once said. This seemed to guarantee our love as invulnerable. Yet, the restlessness of an adolescent sexuality, complicated by the repression of earlier years, was to prove the undoing of our engagement despite our reputation as "a match made in heaven." I soon experienced a strong attraction to my fiancee's sister, and you will seldom find a messier scenario than that. This situation became so volatile that I had to withdraw from the scene completely. Only later were we all able to be reconciled as friends.

In one sense there is no excuse for the risky and hurtful actions described above. Still, there are powerful and normal forces at work in growing up sexually for which easy answers like "the guy's a jerk" or "the lady is a tramp" simply will not do (even my spiritual director counseled me toward the mistake of pursuing my former fiancee's sister). Sex does indeed open windows in our hearts that may unleash destructive winds. Yet, how easily our ministry is founded upon fearful reactions to Hollywood sexual fantasies which define love exclusively in terms of bodily contact, unfaithfulness, "loose" relationships, and selfishness. The spiritual winds which prevail in our sexual encounters may also facilitate spiritual contacts, recommitment, bonding relationships, and generosity in the following ways:

1. Human sexuality clarifies personal values and choices. When Donna and I met in Baltimore, our futures were laid open before us in a uniquely powerful manner. There was "temptation" from one point of view, a near occasion to sin, but there was also revelation in the freeing up of creative possibilities, a near occasion to grace. When we both returned to our chosen paths, having let go of one invitation, the newly discovered fragility of our vocations was accompanied

by the clarification of purpose and personal reinvestment (response-ability) that is the fruit of such "trials."

2. Human sexuality demands and elicits personal commitment. When I made Debbie aware of my interest in her, she was placed in a real dilemma. She liked me, but she loved her sister, Jane. In more subtle circumstances it may have been possible for her to continue relations with both of us. A "neutral" party can manage to maintain friendship with two estranged lovers, but the pitfall and the grace of sexuality lies in its persistence. Sexuality presses for an answer, it demands a commitment. Debbie tried her best to remain a good sister to Jane and a good friend to me, but my sexual self would not let it go at that. I forced her to make a commitment and she made her choice. She elected to stand with her sister. That pledge of loyalty was the gift of so much sexual messiness.

3. Human sexuality draws people together in a powerful way. Sexuality is like a magnet that opposes the human tendency toward isolation and self-absorption. Sex attracts the "I" relentlessly toward "other" and predisposes one sexual pole to the balance and wholeness of the other. This is why the church's gradual recognition of the unitive way (sex is "pro-relational," not primarily pro-creative) as an integral function of intercourse is such an invaluable step toward refashioning our fantasy of love without sex. Far from a one-dimensional physical activity, sex tends toward spirituality, the deepening of intimacy and commitment. This is why it is very difficult to sustain

casual sexual liaisons for long. Immediately such relationships begin to "beg for more," more intimacy which leads to further sexual expression.

4. Human sexuality is pro-creative, overflowing, expansive. Healthy sexuality naturally tends to "reach out and touch someone." The love of a sexual relationship "bursts at its seams" to find expression beyond itself. This is why authentic love breaks out of the limited world of twos into the expansive realm of threes or more. Examples of this truth are the Trinity, Christian communities, and marriages. Jesus described his own participation in this hallmark of true love, a tendency to add to its numbers: "Wherever two or three are gathered in my name, there I am also in their midst." It is in this context that we would review church teaching which prohibits artificial insemination. Couples whose dream of expanding their love has been broken apart by the reality of infertility might be best served by our ability to let go of our fantasy of love without the sex of artificial insemination. Again, the key issue here is the extent of human responsibility for life. It is a matter of whether "artificial" is the correct term for the products of human resourcefulness toward easing pain and fulfilling lifegiving dreams. If such human interventions are integral to God's plan (built in), then "natural" and "holy" would seem more accurate names for them.

In a fantasy world without sex these messy situations might be avoided, but in reality God's love is realized within such ambiguous settings. In fact, if the power of

God's relationship to us is actually defined as sexual
(omni-potent), then we must ask if divine love is fully
available in the asexual (impotent) world of our
fantasies. Sex brings with it messiness, ambiguity, and
hurt, but in so doing it provides for the powerful and
varied possibilities of love. Sex is a force of God's ever
potent love for bringing people together, deepening
their togetherness, and making things happen among
them. Conversely, asexuality is an agent of impotency,
allowing people to be apart and turn inward or
permitting their relationships to stagnate. In this light
we see that celibate love and conjugal love exist in
relational harmony to each other rather than in
opposition. Celibate and married love test, define, and
actualize each other as they express complementary
facets of a divine love that is quite sexual in whatever
personal form it touches us.

Fantasy 2: Love Without Women

It seems to me that our male dominated images of
God and our male dominated ecclesial ministry are
largely a product of our deep seated belief that loving is
a male enterprise, that we are best "kept in love" with
God by male lovers. Stated in another way, a fantasy of
love as an efficient, businesslike undertaking is affirmed
by the male and threatened by the female personality.
We are very afraid that women, with their intuitiveness,
beauty, and passion will either be unequal to the logical
demands of the task, will distract us from our noble
endeavor, or will foul up what we have already
accomplished by "going too far." This fear is so intense

that it has overshadowed mountains of human experience of woman as mother, lover, friend, and partner; experience which clearly reveals the feminine dimension of divine love.

Not only have we refused to allow feminine God-images to penetrate our theology or female ministers to be co-responsible for pastoral leadership, but we long maintained the practice of disguising the femaleness of one key symbol of the femininity of God's care that we had: women religious. The demise of such "habits" and the rise of the women's movement within the church are the beginning of a long and vital struggle to recapture the femininity of God-experience and the centrality of womanly gifts to the success of pastoral ministry. How telling it is that lay women, judged too "unclean" for mainstream ministry, were for years relegated to the pastoral oddjob of parish housekeeping.

The fact that women are emotional in their caring, that they bleed monthly in their capacity to nurture new life, that they are strong in their endurance and unpredictable in their spontaneity all conspire to increase our fear that female participation in spreading God's love will make that enterprise more complex, costly, and ambiguous. We don't pause long enough to consider that God's love is certainly all of those things and it's time that it be symbolized and experienced as such through female leadership in church ministry.

The way of things has always been that it requires male and female, animus and anima, to "make love." More to the point, both man and woman are essential for people to be conceived and born. If ministry is the passion of conceiving divine love and the labor of rebirthing people in God's Spirit, then the very nature of human existence reveals how vital it is that both women and men be co-responsible for its potency. Receiving communion from a female Eucharistic minister, for example, is certainly a sexual encounter, full of a refreshing power and life that was sacrificed (made impotent) by the exile of women from the sanctuary in days past. I do not imply an erotic meaning here, but rather a link between the spiritual experience of being fed and primordial human memories of nourishment. It is our mothers who first feed us from the breast, who first symbolize for us the divine Mother's desire to sustain us. By denying God's people equal access to female ministers, we exile these powerful symbols from our faith along with an integral part of the God we seek to "re-incarnate" as wholly as possible for the world.

This may be the most pressing argument for the ordination of women in the church. We may say what we will, we may play games which simulate the truth, but in the end it is our symbols which mediate God to us. As long as our ministerial symbols are male-dominated, then our image of God will continue to be impoverished and our experience of divine love will be diminished. We will never truly experience the fullness of God's care until all the female ways we experience human care are raised to the spiritual level and "ordained" through official female ministerial leadership in the church. Once our experience of pastoral leadership becomes more female our image of

God can become more feminine also. As our image of God incorporates the female personality, we will be freer to develop more models of womanly leadership in the church. To accomplish all this we need simply adopt a new fantasy: "No love without women!"

Fantasy 3: Love Without Ambiguity

The church long associated divine love with controlled and structured love, so it was natural that the sex act would eventually be marked as legitimately divine only within the borders of married life. With this in mind, there is no small irony in the fact that the process of getting married came to be referred to in society as "settling down." No phrase more succinctly expresses the church's fantasy of love under control without ambiguity. The practice of sex outside of the institution of marriage is labeled as profane for the very reason that it is "uncontrollable" in both cause and effect. Those who experience a movement toward sexual expression within the context of non-marital relationships are counseled to abstain unless or until that drive can be "settled down" within a sacramental structure.

It would be nice if there were three groups of people in the world: couples who choose to get married, celibates who elect not to get married, and singles who are waiting to get married. This simple world, however, is an illusion. We must devise a pastoral strategy for sexuality which includes the messier categories of singles who perceive their status as an ongoing call, divorcees and widows whose marriages come to an abrupt and undesired halt, and celibates who experience a "change of heart" in wanting to marry, often with no corresponding wish to abandon ordained ministry. These are the "easy cases." Our pastoral stance must also address sexuality for the controversial category of gays.

There are two questions to be faced within this increasingly complex sexual arena. The first is the possibility of limiting sex to the institution of marriage, the second is the appropriateness of such a move. Once our formulation of sexual ministry is based on the assumption that sex is pro-relational, we face a real quandary. If sex is the natural expression and nourishment (sacrament) of relationships, and healthy relationships do exist outside marriage (actually these can be healthier than certain marital situations), can sex be confined to marriage? I do not question here the truth that healthy sex involves commitment and that marriage is the ideal setting for the reality of sexual commitment. I raise instead those questions which life itself raises: Is it possible or healthy for everyone to marry? Is it possible for all non-marital relationships to be asexual, lacking genital sexual expression, and still remain healthy?

Our answers to these questions have been more the products of fantasy than of serious engagements with reality. We expect singles to wait for marriage, divorcees to live off the memories of marriage until annulment, and homosexuals to make an "act of will" to become legitimate candidates for marriage. Facing these issues is only a preview of equally complex questions which beg for attention. What about a single or divorced woman who wants to marry, but can only find brief relationships because she is forty and "too old" for a society sold on the idols of youth and beauty? What of the widower who is a "dubious catch" because of his three kids? What of the mentally or physically handicapped who lack skills essential or ideal to marriage? Even if we could convince these lonely, longing souls of our fantasy that sufficient faith and patience will inevitably lead them to love and marriage "if it is God's will," is it pastorally responsible or creative to do so?

A statement from the Vatican on homosexuality referred to gay sexual activity as "behavior to which no one has any conceivable right." Once again, within a fantasy of unambiguous love, who would really argue with the intent of such a declaration? But, in the context of this all-too-real and complex world of ours, we must ask a different question. When we take a look at the tremendous forces of isolation at work in this life, we might ask instead whether an institution has any conceivable right to behavior that denies persons access to the minimal intimacy they need to survive. When such love violates the rights of other people, then it must surely be questioned, but when it violates instead a fantasy of love without ambiguity, then some larger, more humanly pastoral issues must take precedence. As the church contends with the thorny problems of homosexuality and child abuse within the ordained ministry, the connection between such sad stories and false pastoral ideals should not be lost upon us.

Fantasy 4: Love Without Revolution

Several years into her first marriage, my wife, Marlene, felt that things were not going well and approached her parish priest seeking guidance. His response to her concerns was a reassurance that she was making too much of trivial matters. She should not worry, but go home and be a good wife and everything would work out. A few years later that relationship ended in divorce.

I use the word "revolution" here to indicate, not rebellion, but turning (change, movement, conversion, journey). People who have "settled in" find love easier, more manageable. When lovers decide to compromise the community of interpersonal conversion for the commonality of impersonal uniformity, a kind of peace may prevail, but it is one of mutual stagnation rather than vibrancy. The church is on a journey; God's children are a pilgrim people. The challenge before the community is to avoid the temptation of becoming "settlers" and accept the normalcy of the journey. For Christians there is something amiss if we are stationary for too long, if the healthy movement of the one or the few does not call the other or the many to "join the revolution."

On the terrain of interpersonal relationships this constant migration is a source of both tension and possibility. When a husband or wife remarks: "You're not the person I married," they are expressing the ambiguity brought on by a revolution in their relationship (one or both have changed). If there is an openness and engagement toward these changes a "new couple" may well emerge out of the "new person." If there is anger and denial, a domineering spouse may succeed in burying the issues in order to reinforce the fragile peace of the status quo. Finally, a third possibility is that the "revolutionary" spouse, too strong to accept the repression of valid issues, takes a firm stand for personal integrity. This is where the positive possibilities of revolution become the last resort of rebellion, often resulting in separation or divorce.

Love would be convenient and easy if people never changed, if they always changed together, or if they sacrificed personal growth in favor of a communal status quo. These scenarios, however, are a fantasy. Not only is change a human reality, it is a spiritual necessity. How sad it is to realize the many times individual spouses have been counseled to give up the journey, to "stay home" and be good, rather than risk rocking the boat of their marriages, as my wife was encouraged to do by the priest. I think most of us have known people who have "settled" for the false security of love without revolution and have witnessed the light going out in their eyes. Their marriages continue to exist at the expense of their personal turning or conversion. We have also met people who have remained true to the journey at the cost of their marriages. Contrary to unfortunate stereotypes, there is often great struggle and mourning over such decisions. Yet, we can also name couples who have established a mutual commitment to personal revolution and realize that the best marriages are a product of such a courageous investment.

Many of the church's marriage laws are based on this fantasy of love without revolution. The manner in which the church has treated those who have left ordained ministry or religious life because of personal transitions also reflects this illusion. The fact that men and women in love do change as they face life's challenges should not ostracize them from the community or from their ministries. In Ireland the people have voted to outlaw divorce. The sadness in this is its symbolism of the tenacity of fantasies of love without movement. The reality is that people are often getting divorced for the very reason that they presumed "marriage is forever": It was taken for granted that "things will always be the same." No amount of denial in the form of civil or religious legislation will cover up the truth of personal change in love.

People will always take "final vows" in religious orders and make "indissoluble" marriage bonds. Yet, the final truth is that all such unions have human elements which must be subject to the only truly permanent commitment we make: the commitment to the Lord. This is the only authentically "final vow." Our task is to emphasize pastoral strategies that will allow our many loves to reflect the permanency of that divine-human relationship. It is toward that goal that we now make some closing remarks.

Right-Brained Love

I was in a donut shop one Sunday, standing in line behind a mother with a small boy. As they were preparing to leave, the boy wandered over to a corner of the shop and began eyeing a big chocolate donut behind the glass case. He looked at his mother as he pointed at the donut and asked if he could have it. She reassured him that she had one of those already tucked away in her bag. This did not make the slightest impression on the kid, and as his mother turned to walk toward the door he burst into tears. The mother went over and over her logical explanation of why they didn't need that particular donut. Still the youth kept pointing and bawling. After a few minutes you could almost see comicbook thought bubbles forming over everyone else's heads: "Forget logic and buy the kid that donut." Instead, the mother dragged the screaming boy out the door, sure that she was right.

Jack Shea tells a similar story in which a little girl on a plane thinks she is upside down because she sees that the clouds, which have always been above her, are now below. In this case a gruff old cigar smoker comes to the rescue by saying: "We are upside down—but it's alright." The story ends with the little girl climbing into his lap. As ministers of divine love we might be the facilitators of a lot more lap climbing if we balance our logical left brain with our intuitive right in loving God's own.

If You Don't Look Good, We Don't Look Good

The healing process for my wife after her divorce has been a gradual but steady one. A few years ago we were spending some intimate time together and as we touched she remarked how good I looked. I returned her compliment, but noticed that she turned away. When I asked her what was wrong she replied: "I don't look that good" (actually she looked great, but "beauty is in the eye of the beholder," and she was the beholder in this instance). She still felt strains of personal ugliness from her divorce. At that point we had to pause until I shared with her my feelings and experiences of her beauty. Only then could our lovemaking continue.

Such is the challenge of a ministry of love in messy times. So many people have been through terrible experiences which have left them feeling dirty, have robbed them of their self esteem. When the minister comes along it seems to be impossible to "make love" to such people until they are brought to the point where they feel worthy of love's attention. The first step for the minister, then, may be to surface memories and experiences of personal worth and beauty for the person. From that point on it will be possible to create a real "love-making" experience.

I think it's the Vidal Sasson commercial that uses the phrase: "If you don't look good, we don't look good." It seems a particularly appropriate line with which to end this chapter. We live in an age where the quest for personal beauty is at an all time high. Beauty aids, exercise videos, and ads for cosmetic surgery are everywhere. We have created a society in which a youthful and perfect appearance is the mark of acceptability and lovability. The strong message is that cosmetic beauty is the key to being loved by self and others.

We can easily criticize such trends and label them as vain, secular pursuits as we pretend to stand above them. Yet, has not the church been guilty of creating standards of spiritual perfection that have many ties to such attitudes? Have we at times created a race of spiritual anorexics who never quite feel worthy of the love we offer unless they change something about themselves? Have some of our ministries been marked with subtle messages which suggest spiritual cosmetic surgery as the condition for divine or ecclesial love?

In the end the criterion by which we might evaluate our ministry is the extent to which people feel good about themselves, about God, and about life, when they leave us. If they feel dirty or ugly, unworthy or discouraged, when they conclude their contact with us, it may indicate something about the quality of our caring and the task of reshaping such ministry. If they don't look good to themselves because of us, then our ministry will certainly not look good. If those in need of love's healing can see in our eyes the reflection of all they can be in God's sight, rather than a picture of their own keenly felt shortcomings, they will be much more likely to respond with life and growth. It is in this way that they will become effective lovers themselves and can be our partners in transforming the world into a place full of divine love. Then, instead of losing our love on the rocks, we will be the rock, like Peter, in whom the Lord has established a sign that the love of God is for all and forever.

Items for Individual Reflection/Group Process

1. Recall an experience when your fantasy of love was "blown apart." What was lost? What was gained? Did the wind of the Spirit prove to be present? What direction did it blow?

2. Has the church's fantasy of "love without sex" influenced your sexuality? Has that fantasy held any benefits for you? What elements of the fantasy have led to repression and stagnation in your personal/pastoral development?

3. What is your position on the future of women in the church? As the ecclesial fantasy of "love without women" is blown apart, where will the wind of the Spirit take us? Identify the pastoral losses of a male dominated church ministry.

4. What has been the role of Marian devotion in salvaging what little importance we have afforded to the place of women in God's plan? How might the future of Marian devotion be a source of a new faith in the indispensable role of women for ministry?; for witnessing the fullness of God's love?

5. Can sexual love be confined to marital relationships without harming or inflicting injustice upon love's poor (singles, gays, divorced, etc.)? How do you define "sexual love"? In what ways does the expansion of love to the unitive way (an expression of lovemaking as much as baby-making) change the presumptions which dictate our ministry in this regard?

6. How would you counsel a gay person with regard to his/her sex life? Knowing that gays are normal human beings, in that they desire and need love and affirmation, how could such needs be creatively fulfilled? How have our present approaches failed?

7. What does the reality of our high divorce rate say about the "mobility" of love? To what extent are church marriage laws subtle versions of Irish laws which deny the reality of marital

breakdown? How might church ministries which have faced and responded to divorce be compared to the ministry of Mother Theresa who has confronted death by devoting her life, not to reality denial, but to processing death with dignity?

8. Do you agree that all human commitments must "take a back seat" to our commitment to the Lord? How are we to know when our commitments represent a "conflict of interests"?

9. The church has counseled those who suffer the pain of infertility to "turn to religion instead of science" (artificial insemination) for an answer to their dilemma. What does such advice infer about God, the purpose of religion, and the role of ministry in loving the world? Is there better counsel?

Activities for Pastoral Staffs/Ministries

1. The parish staff or religious education board might evaluate the
   state of sex education in the parish or community and draw up
   fresh or follow-up programs accordingly. The
   philosophy/theology spoken by whatever program is developed
   should be carefully heeded. If no sex education has been
   undertaken, perhaps this indicates its own message and need.

2. Ministers to the broken-hearted, divorced, widowed, orphaned,
   etc. (those "fallen out of love") can plan time to ponder and
   celebrate their work. A key question might be the approach taken
   to the pain they encounter. Does their ministry tend to be in a
   hurry to put people back together again rather than allowing
   them to be "blown apart"? Is there an impatience for the
   wounded to get on with their lives or is there a willingness to wait
   for the wind of the Spirit to blow?

3. Plan a parish or community celebration for those who have
   symbolized the fidelity of divine love amidst broken relationships.
   Single parents, for example, could be gathered to "renew their
   vows," their heroic commitment to witnessing true parental love
   in the face of divorce or abandonment.

4. Those who minister to engaged or married couples through
   Pre-Cana, Encounter, or other programs can use the material in
   this chapter/book to reflect upon and evaluate their ministry from
   another perspective.

5. Make a list of the "lost loves" of your life: relationships, departed
   relatives and friends, dreams and fantasies, possessions, etc.
   Discuss how these losses have matured your faith and ministry.
   What have you found in the midst of your losses? Share your
   discoveries with the group.

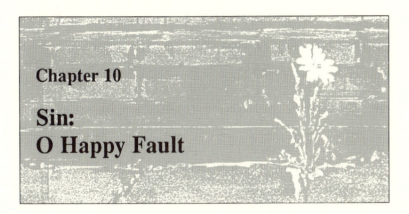

Chapter 10

Sin:
O Happy Fault

"O happy fault; O necessary sin of Adam!"
— The Exultet

I must have been about nine or ten when I first started
to develop scruples. Fall was upon the city of Denver
and winter was fast approaching. The dropping
temperatures were a blessing for me, however, because
they gave me natural access to an inconspicuous place
to hide my growing list of sins: my winter coat pocket. I
don't recall how it got started or in what manner it grew
out of proportion to reality, but my first memory of the
list is linked to feelings of panic and desperation. The
numbers of the usual childhood confession items
(disobedience, lying, impure thoughts, fighting) had
mushroomed into the hundreds and my plan of carefully
"budgeting" these sins over several months' confessions

seemed doomed. Like a debtor whose installment plan is jeopardized by the arrival of unexpected bills, the balance of my ledger was growing faster than I could make payments.

The bathroom in the hall behind the kitchen was my secret hideaway for tallying up the list each week and doing a little private stewing about its magnitude. Whether I had just been to confession and had to lower the totals or had begun another "reign of terror" and needed to do some addition, the bathroom seemed a safe and appropriate place. If only I had seen the wisdom of flushing the list down the toilet along with my other internal waste. The symbolic import of my hideout, however, did not occur to me at such a tender age.

It was both a trying and comforting day when my redemption arrived. As I was making my usual careful exit from the bathroom, I prepared to slip the list into my coat pocket which hung conveniently in the hall on the way to the kitchen. I had this routine down to a science which enabled me to get my list into the pocket without even breaking stride. I leaned down and pushed the paper halfway into the pocket when my heart jumped. Through the hall window I caught a glimpse of my mother working at the kitchen sink. Realizing it was too late to retreat I acted as if everything was normal and finished my task with as much subtlety as I could muster.

When I got to the kitchen my fears were confirmed. Mom had seen the paper and wanted to know what it was. Repeated denials were useless; she knew the paper existed. The miraculous thing, though, was her refusal to simply go retrieve the list herself. She desired my trust more than she sought my guilt or that paper. In the end that may have made all the difference. In any case, I finally gave in to her persistence and showed her the list. We then had a long and wonderful talk which resulted in the disposal of the list and the first tentative steps on the road to my earliest childhood memory of a real conversion in my image of God in relation to the notion of sin.

Examining Our Corporate Christian Conscience

I tell this story as I begin a discussion on sin because it points to key elements of our Christian identity and value system prior to the Second Vatican Council. Scrupulosity may be born of a psychological predisposition, but it is nurtured and sustained in a religious environment permeated with the values of perfection and control. My desperation as a child stemmed from a self-image tarnished by a growing perception of myself as both messy (imperfect) and powerless to do anything about it (out of control). Healing came when my mother took the time to filter out some of the unhealthy overtones of my personal/communal value system and balance them with messages of acceptance and support.

So it is that our communal sense of sin shapes the content of our ministry to it, a ministry of evangelization and reconciliation. In turn, the way we go about evangelizing and reconciling influences our understanding of sin. It is vital, then, to pay attention to our definition of sin by constantly asking some questions: Is that definition accurate according to our tradition and experience? Does it give rise to a ministry that facilitates reconciliation and conversion, that is, makes the world better and brings the Kingdom nearer? Finally, does our ministry to sinners continue to support and fashion a healthy understanding and attitude toward sin among the people? With our goal of practicing effective ministry in a messy world as a backdrop, we now address those questions.

Just prior to Vatican II we pretty much had sin figured out. There was Original sin, a kind of generic sin which brought us all under evil's influence. There were mortal and venial sins, each with clearly defined identifying marks. There existed heaven, hell, and limbo so that we would know exactly where to place the various categories of sinners. There were sacraments to deal with the different types of sin and two brands of grace, sanctifying and actual, to help ward off the effects of evil. Lastly, there were explanations for the difficult questions all this neatness surfaced. The problem of evil, for example, was explained as God's way of testing us: "Job's been good for a while, but what will happen if I turn up the heat a little?" If there was any doubt about where an individual would end up, the death bed provided the final answers. Everyone was given one last chance to save the day or blow it with their dying breath.

We are developing the wisdom to see that sin is not so neatly identified and dispatched. Modern theologians are assisting us in reflecting upon the complexities and subtleties of evil in our midst. A review of some of their insights is the first step toward realizing that ministry to sinfulness (reconciliation and evangelization) must sometimes be as complex as is sin itself.

1. Sin Is Not Easily Defined

It was a few years ago in a class at Loyola that Tad Guzie suggested that much of what we have traditionally referred to as sin may actually be the process of growing up. Such a statement has numerous consequences for pastoral practice, among them being an inquiry into the wisdom of legislating the Sacrament of Reconciliation for primary-age children. It is not my purpose here to review such practices in detail, but to point out that many of them are based upon assumptions regarding sin and evil that may be questionable.

I recall an incident which occurred at home while our boys were in the bathroom brushing their teeth. The two of them were playfully getting ready for bed when Mark's toothbrush suddenly came flying out of the room. In an "age of reason" I may have quickly identified this seven-year-old's act as that of a deliberately disobedient "bad boy." Ministering to sinners in life's mess, however, demands further investigation before such an act can be named as "sin." When I asked Mark why he threw his toothbrush he looked at me and shrugged, "I don't know." His action may have been an unreflective impulse, a test of boundaries, or his way of exploring the world of right and wrong. It seems to me that in the process of growing up many children, adolescents, and adults find themselves in situations which elicit similarly ambiguous responses. It is not our priority to apply convenient labels to such acts, but to explore them carefully with a view toward reconciliation and conversion.

2. Sin Involves an Ideal

In his book, *Morality and Its Beyond*, Dick Westley makes an important distinction between sin and morality. Morality, he writes, involves the requirement to avoid any evil which inflicts harm upon myself or others. Sin, however, is a failure to live up to a Christian ideal. Put another way, to be moral is to be good (stay in line), but to be sinless is to be great (shatter the lines by enfleshing new standards of life-giving and love-making in Christ). Following the rules like the Pharisees will not make me a saint because it does not require me to foster the Lord's dream for the world. God wants us to do more than behave ourselves; the Lord desires for us to build up the possibility of the Kingdom.

When this point is translated into the metaphor of these writings, we realize that it is not enough for the followers of Jesus to avoid making a mess. Instead, they must actively seek to make something beautiful of the world. This too introduces ambiguity and complexity into our dealings with sin. How do we educate people beyond the repentance that "cries over spilt milk" to repenting our failures to risk pouring ourselves out for each other? Minimum daily requirements are easily measured and met; transgressions against an ideal are more subtle and complex. So too will be the nature of our ministry to sinners in a messy world.

3. Sin Is Not Puny

Matthew Fox has illustrated that one of the shortcomings of our Christian upbringing in regards to sin was the tacit assumption that sin is puny. This happened because we were taught as children to confess the small sins like disobedience and impure thoughts, but were never trained to realize the magnitude of sin as we grew into adulthood. The result is that many adults still confess the minor sins of their youth while remaining oblivious or passive in the face of the real evils that influence their behavior and afflict their communities (violence, materialism, racism, etc.). It is this dichotomy which creates some of the angriest, most vocal critics of church endeavors into peace, justice, and economic issues from the ranks of our most faithful churchgoers.

Once again, those evils which loom largely on the horizons of our souls are ever so subtle and difficult to tame. It is much more comforting to deal with those sinful commodities which can be easily listed and dispatched because of their manageable size. To truly become a minister to sinners amid life's mess, however, requires that we heed the Lord's counsel to forget about the splinters in our eyes until we first deal with the beams.

4. Sin Is the Problem, Not Sins

Rahner's introduction of the "fundamental option" as the measure of good or evil in a person was the dawn of a new age in evangelization. It was the beginning of a time when we were challenged to put away the calculator and pay attention to the heart when discerning our need for conversion. Just as the forest can get lost while studying the trees, so too can the meaning of a life be overlooked because of too great an emphasis on isolated actions. Jesus, in his defense of the woman who washed his feet with her tears, illustrated how the application of this truth actually effects the reconciliation it proclaims: "I tell you, then, the great love she has shown proves that her many sins have been forgiven. But whoever has been forgiven little shows only a little love" (Luke 7/47).

This too is a much messier way of ministering to a sinful world. It takes more work to study a life than to scrutinize isolated actions. And while the larger vision is a truer one, seeing it requires more patience, scrutiny, and interaction. This is why the Catechumenate has replaced convert class as the model for Christian initiation. Thankfully, this wholistic approach to conversion is based in part upon a recognition that seemingly simpler times created messes of their own, as illustrated by my childhood struggles with scrupulosity.

Naming the Foundation of Evil

Where does all this leave us? Certainly I do not mean to say that the naming of sin is now arbitrary or that confronting it is relatively unimportant. On the contrary, the goal is to name sin more accurately and to confront it with increasing effectiveness. Focusing our awareness of the complexity of this task should ultimately support the church's mission of evangelization and reconciliation.

By conserving the energy we once expended upon misnomers (sins that were really matters of growth), minimum requirements (being good rather than being great), red herrings (puny sins rather than pervasive evils), and distractions (isolated actions rather than life directions), we should have more resources to name and treat the real evils that afflict us. Perhaps no starting point would be more helpful in this enterprise than that of naming the basic sin that lies at the root of all others. I will suggest two interrelated evils, two sides of one dark coin, to which all other sin may be traced. I hope to illustrate how these evils are related to the temptation of neatness over the challenge of confronting the messiness and ambiguity of sin.

A. Narcissism: I Am the Only One

I suspect narcissism as the root of all evil. Narcissism claims that "I am the only one," that the world revolves around me, that all decisions are made in relation to their effect upon me. Anyone who travels a lot has encountered numerous people who drive the road as if they are alone, as oblivious to their precarious impact upon others as they are unyielding to those who get in their way. As spiritual voyagers we need not be overly astute to recognize the danger, annoyance, and destructiveness wrought by those who journey the road of life in similar fashion.

Narcissism is a creeping kind of evil that seeps into our bones gradually and becomes very easy to rationalize because it resembles other healthy human qualities like assertiveness, self-awareness, and individuality. The evil of narcissism is also a social disease in that it is bred and supported in the attitudes of families, communities, and nations. In other words, a group or nation can also become the "I" of the universe at the expense of other groups and nations.

Narcissism is so very messy to deal with because it is ultimately rooted in the temptation of neatness. What is more tidy than treating all of life on the basis of its influence upon me? Decisions about what to think, say, and do become easy when they can all be made on the basis of my personal world or the world of a group. Narcissism is also rather difficult to confront because, true to the image of its progenitor, it is born of a preoccupation with a vision of personal loveliness. In that sense it is a challenge to distract the narcissist from the "beatific vision" long enough to unmask the ugly destructiveness of such a neat little world.

Four examples of narcissism in action help reveal how all evil is rooted in this basic sin. Each of these cases describes a narcissistic approach to life's crises, issues, or challenges. These examples also illustrate how the

movement toward narcissism often begins with a
healthy desire to redress a wrong, clean up a messy
situation, or make life better in general. The end result,
however, is usually worse than the first. Readers are
invited to dig up the narcissistic roots of the sinful
situations in their own lives.

Example 1

A few years ago a friend of mine sought counseling in
order to sort out some unresolved issues from her past.
These matters were seriously affecting her physical and
emotional health. Eventually the counselor concluded
that the main issues at stake involved the woman's
relationship with her mother. The counselor maintained
that these unresolved feelings would have to be brought
to her mother's attention. My friend related to me her
reservations about the wisdom of this procedure but
submitted to the advice of her counselor. In a stormy
and painful session she confronted her mother with her
inmost self. Since that time their relationship has
become increasingly strained and guilt over the
confrontation has overshadowed whatever inner healing
it might have accomplished for my friend.

What happened, I believe, is that the counselor fell
into the narcissistic trap of treating her patient as an
individual instead of in relationship with her mother. In
other words, the emotions and hurts of the mother were
shelved as she was used like a dartboard to receive all
the unresolved feelings of her daughter. No one was
there to mediate the world of the mother, to translate
her daughter's painful message into words that could be

heard. What happened that day was not communication, but a soliloquy. The end result was further alienation rather than reconciliation. A neat, narcissistic solution produced a bigger mess.

Example 2

Narcissism may be a chief cause of the high divorce rate. It seems to me that the seeds of such a divorce are planted when one spouse responds to the complex challenge of marriage with a narcissistic solution. The spouse in question concludes that the marriage can be simplified and improved by making the "we" into an "I." One partner, for example, begins to dominate the marriage by subsuming the personality of the other into his own. What "we want" out of marriage becomes, in effect, what "I want." This dubious interpretation of the unity theme of marriage is common enough that we might do well to replace the popular unity candle ritual at our Christian weddings with a more healthy symbol of the delicate balance of individuality and partnership in marriage. It is well to bear in mind the familiar joke: "Couples are in agreement that 'the two should become one'; the problem arises when they try to decide which one."

Example 3

The abortion issue is a thorny problem which is plagued with an overabundance of neatly narcissistic solutions. Pro-life groups take the side of the fetus (the infant is the only one) without due consideration of the mother while pro-choice groups take the side of the mother (the woman is the only one) at the expense of the unborn fetus. The church does well to promote the value of new life and the truth that such life is born at the cost of pain and sacrifice. This teaching, however, needs to be balanced by an investment in feminine concerns over a woman's physical and psychological health, integrity of conscience, and stewardship of the body. The most creative, lifegiving solutions to the abortion issue are those complex enough to consider the interrelationship of the mother, the fetus, and the world into which an infant is to be born. If the church is serious about challenging abortion it is advisable for us to reformulate overly tidy teachings on birth control.

Example 4
Dogmatism is religion's form of narcissism. Dogmatism claims a monopoly on truth. Even worse, it proclaims that truth is possessed by individuals or individual groups, usually in a hierarchical structure. Ecclesial dogmatism is at the heart of the destructive clash among the triangle of church life: the hierarchy, the theologians, and the laity. It is never proper for one point of the triangle to claim truth over and above the others. Truth emerges from the communal interrelationship of the entire Body of Christ rather than from attempts of one part of the Body to prevail over the others. Recent actions against theologians Charles Curran, Leonardo Boff, and Matthew Fox, in which power has been employed to reassert the possession and control of truth are overly neat. Paradoxically, these moves have caused more ambiguity

for the laity than might have resulted from a commitment to more complex and communal approaches to the search for truth.

B. Passivity: It Doesn't Matter

Passivity is the second deadly sin of our age. Of course, I am not using this term in the valid and vital monastic sense of receptivity to divine action. The sin of passivity to which I refer is a distortion of valid Christian notions like submission to God's will (let it be) and hope (things will work out). We seem to have taught people well that "God will provide," but we don't seem to have communicated the integral role which people play in that provision. There are far too many Christians around today whose positive faith in God has left them with the conclusion that "it (their effort) doesn't matter." We have done much too good a job convincing people that their "puny efforts" are rather trivial and that it is God who saves the day. We can see folks demonstrate such faith every week at Sunday Liturgy. Once a parish where I worked held a ceremony for its Confirmation class at a Sunday Mass. I had to ask four Confirmation families before one agreed to perform the simple task of bringing up the gifts. Such incidents seem trivial, but they are indicative of engrained attitudes which rear their ugly heads at other times when much more is at stake.

Passivity is the flip side of the sin of narcissism, its logical conclusion. Increasing involvement with self leads to decreasing involvement with others. It is narcissistic thought, increasingly prevalent in religious as well as secular circles, which leads to the rationalization of human pain via the canonization of passive philosophies like "that's life" (secular) and "it's God's will" (religious). Only a thin line separates such attitudes, whether calculated or naive, from the nihilism of "it doesn't matter" (nothing matters). Today's scramble for money is indicative of our compulsive self-preoccupation aimed at total independence and isolation from the needs of community. From this standpoint, state lotteries may be a leading candidate for a national sacrament of evil in that they symbolize what they effect (narcissism) and effect what they symbolize (passivity).

The temptation to passivity is also a temptation to a false sense of neatness. It is always easier and cleaner to let the next person do it, especially in a faith context where "the next person" is God. We all dread involvement ("I don't want to get involved") precisely because of the personal complications it entails. If we are to deal with the sin of passivity in our midst we must begin to appreciate how very essential our participation is to quality of life and the coming of the Kingdom.

A few years ago a news story captured headlines across the country. A woman was gang raped in a bar. The significant thing about this incident, however, was the fact that no one stepped in to protest or put a stop to the crime. On the contrary, reports indicated that a number of bystanders actually cheered on the rapists. Events like this echo the holocaust. They are tragedies that call us to wonder: "How could this happen?" A more precise rendering of that question for our purposes would be: "How could people allow this to happen?"

Society's children allow such things to happen because they have been taught to "hang loose," to "play it cool," and to "never sweat the small stuff." They occur in a culture lulled into isolation and complacency by television, advertising, and the news media. Such things take place when the watchwords of a generation like "I'm okay, you're okay" are gradually translated into "everything's okay" or "nothing's wrong." These things happen when pessimistic or fatalistic attitudes create feelings of helplessness or despair. Avoidable tragedies will continue to plague us as long as the news media, in search of rating points, promotes a hellish vision of the world which sends people into fearful, passive withdrawal. The overtones of personal "irresponse-ability" and fatalism in such broadcasts is captured by ironic conclusions like Walter Cronkite's "That's the way it is!"

God's children permit such tragedies to happen when the church allows sacraments, the sources of our power for good, to become idols. An idol is a false god that we worship for its perceived power to save us. A sacrament becomes a false god when we receive it for its power to do things for us rather than celebrating it to participate in God's power to change the world. In short, a sacrament is an idol when it makes us idle or passive. Ironically, the pre-Vatican II rite of Confession promoted both narcissism (private box, private God) and passivity (everything's wrong; don't do anything).

So, the sin of passivity is a direct result of an improper theology which made sacraments into things to be received for personal profit rather than actions to be shared for the transformation of the world in the power of God. Like the money sought from the lottery, the grace of the sacraments can be pursued for purposes of isolation and passivity.

Such a misguided theology is a natural consequence of the church's past efforts at "marketing" sacraments, creating needs by identifying humanity as wretched and helpless. When our evangelization labels people as "bad" (God-orphans), they become passive consumers, gobbling up graces in order to save themselves. When our evangelizing names people as "good" (God-children), they become co-creators, participating in grace in order to save the world in Christ.

To the extent that sacraments continue to be idols, people will go on being idle or passive, church rites will be used for narcissistic purposes like "saving my soul," and the mess that we wish to remove will continue to plague us. To the extent that we call people to realize their best selves in the image of their creator, people will be activated for others and will participate in the creative transformation of a messy world into the Kingdom. Folks inevitably show up on Ash Wednesday to ritualize their messiness and on Easter to symbolize their escape from it, but the Easter Vigil can only truly be celebrated by those who have walked the dusty road of Lent inbetween.

A great obstacle we face in confronting the evil of human passivity is our penchant for discouraging full participation in church life as a whole. It is difficult to challenge voluntary passivity when our models of leadership and authority facilitate a kind of enforced passivity. Too many laity have learned that their efforts, concerns, and feelings don't really count ("it doesn't matter") by the way pastors and pastoral ministers hold onto power over parishes and programs. These people are understandably reluctant to "spring into action" on those occasions when their contributions are suddenly "urgently required." The Chicago diocesan newspaper recently reported that area seminaries are beginning to teach collaborative leadership skills. This is welcome news for a church desperately in need of a less token, more integral lay investment in ministry toward the demise of the sin of passivity in the world.

A Happy Fault

Perhaps what we have lost in our flight from sin and our quest for perfection is that part of our faith expressed in the Exultet at the Easter Vigil: "O happy fault; O necessary sin of Adam, which gained for us so great a Redeemer!" Strange as it seems, it remains the Christian sensibility to actually celebrate the consequences of sin even as we confess them. Perhaps we need to be reminded more often that the heights of God's love are measured most truly against the depths of the world's shortcomings and that the triumphs of human virtue are made possible and gloious only within the context of limitation and struggle. More will be said about this in the final chapter. For now, suffice it to say that this deficiency in our appreciation of sin is highlighted each year by our celebration of All Saints Day after our neglect, if not disdain, for what we term the secular observance of Halloween. Indeed, the haste with which this festival is rejected by fundamentalists as Satanic rather than integrated as the flip side to our ritual of saintliness is evidence of our predilection for projecting our shadow rather than owning and celebrating it. As long as this continues to be the case, we might wonder if we will ever truly understand God's love and its power in our lives to dispel the darkness of sin: "Darkness vanishes forever!"

Items for Individual Reflection/Group Process

1. Did scrupulosity touch your life as a child? To what degree? What did that experience say about your image of God and the church's understanding of ministry at the time?

2. When you examine your conscience, what are you looking for? How do you define sin as an adult? How has that sense of sin changed since you were a child?

3. Have you graduated from the school of "puny sin"? Do you spend time and energy addressing the tiny faults of your life? Are you able to dig down to the roots of the evil in your life and in society? What are those roots?

4. Are you able to separate the basic orientation of your life (fundamental option) from the individual acts (sins) which you commit? Does this distinction confuse or clarify the issue of sin in your life? Why? How do you know when an action has become a deeper orientation? What is the challenge of this distinction for the church's ministry of reconciliation and evangelization?

5. Do you agree that narcissism and passivity constitute the basic evils of our time? Is there any sin which cannot be traced to this two-sided evil? How do narcissism and passivity influence you? Where do they show up in your behavior?

6. The recent Notre Dame study of liturgy found that, while most Catholics have accepted the changes of Vatican II, they have done so without much enthusiasm. Is our reluctance to embrace Vatican II's participatory style of liturgy related to the sin of passivity in our day? How?

7. Are sacraments in your parish celebrated as actions? Have they instead become idols (idles)? How can this attitude be challenged in a community? What is the role of liturgical ministry in confronting narcissism and passivity?

8. Have you ever bought a lottery ticket? What would happen to you if you won? How would your life be different? Would it be better or worse, richer or poorer? What are people really hoping for when they buy a lottery ticket? Is this something worth hoping for? Can it be a sin to buy a lottery ticket?

9. Is sin necessary for salvation? Why or why not? How does the line from the Exultet, "O happy fault; O necessary sin of Adam...," strike you? In what sense are your faults "happy?"

Activities for Pastoral Staffs/Ministries

1. Two eighth graders were caught with pornographic materials. The minister, wanting to nip the problem in the bud, planned to contact the parents immediately. One boy begged her not to, for he was sure he would be beaten if his parents knew. A parent of the other boy simply said: "boys will be boys." Share similar stories to establish the connectedness of evil in your community. Devise strategies for "breaking the chain" of sin.

2. Organize study/discussion groups around the Bishops' Pastorals on Peace and the Econcomy. Pay attention to the tenor of the discussions (anger, openness, resistance, or excitement) as a barometer of where things stand and what follow-up work is necessary. A peace and justice committe can be formed out of these discussion groups if none exists.

3. Those responsible for the various types of Penance services in the parish might evaluate the way in which the sacrament of Reconciliation is celebrated. What messages does this style of celebration speak with regard to communal notions of sin and forgiveness? What changes can be implemented that will express the desired sense of reconciliation?

4. Money is a key element in the narcissism of our age. Finance committees might review money matters in the parish with a view toward modeling Christian stewardship to the community. Does the seeking and use of money serve people (outreach) or does it tend to preoccupy pastoral time and effort (self-absorption)?

5. Name some modern fictional works in which the characters are portrayed as complex, a mixture of vice and virtue. Contrast these to the heroes of old, who were usually portrayed as totally pure and above compromise. Discuss the healthy elements of this shift in our image of heroism. Point out some of the liabilities. One

such negative is modern society's suggestion that it's unfashionable to be nice, while it's admirable to be wicked, a la J.R. Ewing in "Dallas" or Alexis in "Dynasty."

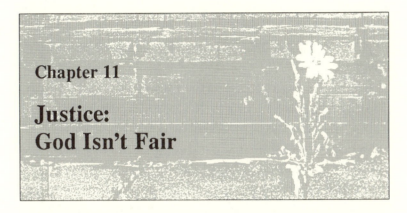

Chapter 11

Justice:
God Isn't Fair

Today you are the law; not some book, not the lawyers, not a marble
statue or the trappings of the court. Those are just symbols of our
desire to be just. They are, in fact, a prayer; a fervent and a
frightened prayer. In my religion they say: 'Act as if you have faith
and faith will be given to you.' If we are to have faith in justice, we
need only to believe in ourselves and act with justice. You see, I
believe there is justice in our hearts."
— from the film: *The Verdict*

I have done some exceedingly naive things in my life.
Yet, like many people, my blunders have not stemmed
simply from stupidity, but from a learned idealism about
life and its workings. Several years ago, when I was in
the thick of one of the roughest periods of my life, I was
called to jury duty. I had been parking my car at the
train station and taking public transportation to court.
On the third day of duty I was running behind and was

worried about the possibility of being late. When I got to the station there were no parking places left and the train was already pulling in. I frantically searched for a place, but there were none to be found. Since I had only an instant to make a decision I quickly turned into a "no parking" zone and, operating on my instinctive convictions about proper priorities, about what is ultimately "right," I ran to the train.

I didn't think much about the incident during the day. I felt good about making the train and being on time. I called my wife just before leaving court and it was she who began to pull me back to reality by voicing her misgivings about what might await me at the train station. As I stepped onto the platform I immediately realized that her dire prophecies had been fulfilled because my car was nowhere in sight. I had been expecting a ticket, but I received a bonus in the form of a tow! It began to rain and I called Marlene for a ride to the police station.

My explanations about the situation, my complaints about inadequate parking at the station, and my punctuality for court duty made no difference. I had to pay my parking ticket, go retrieve my car from a remote towing "service," and pay the towing fee. It was a lousy time for me anyway and the added insult of having to walk through dog shit to retrieve my vehicle served as a symbol of everything else I was going through at the time. In my fatigue and frustration I cried in the car as I drove home. My tears were certainly "a cry for justice."

The God Who Doesn't Play Fair

It is in such ways that we learn the hard truth that life is not fair. Indeed, we have grown very fond of quoting that overused question to those who suffer life's injustice: "Who said life was fair?" (Who said that saying life isn't fair makes it any easier to suffer injustice?) In the context of faith and ministry, however, it is necessary to go one step further. It is not enough to come to grips with the unfairness of life. We must begin our struggle for justice with the bold and unflinching proclamation that God, as the author of life as we know it, is also unfair from a certain faith perspective. God is quite unjust.

The ministry of justice in a messy world dawns, gains its impetus and integrity, in the admission that God is unjust. This is a hard starting point for those who have been raised on the "just God theory," the notion that our Lord lives and breathes, desires and enfleshes justice in our world. Now, by no means is it an asset to our ministry to question the Lord's commitment to and participation in justicemaking. Yet, we must acknowledge the liabilities that mission has suffered historically due to overly pious and passive notions of how it is accomplished. If we were to devise a caricature to describe our sense of Jesus as justice- maker, it might be the image of superman: "...strange visitor from another kingdom who came to this world with powers and abilities far beyond those of mere mortals;...and who disguised as Jesus of Nazareth, mild mannered carpenter from a remote Galilean village, fights a neverending battle for truth, justice, and the Christian way!"

The Roots for Our "Fair-Mindedness"

Such an image may seem outlandish, but the pervasiveness of our idealism about justice in growing up and the gravity of our struggle to come to terms with the failure of God to make life fair testifies to the measure of truth it holds. The origin of this ill-advised faith in a God who "plays fair" is quite traceable. It starts in childhood, where all "good parents" respond to our felt need for fairness by creating a just world within the home. We see them pour soft drinks evenly, give Christmas gifts equally, and dispense privileges in careful proportion to our age and maturity. When we play games we discover that we can redress many grievances with a hearty shout of "no fair!" Much to our delight, we find that we can often obtain our way, which to us is also the just way, by bawling as loudly and annoyingly as possible.

Television and movies further deepen our childhood conditioning to presume that stories end happily and justice prevails. What child could spend hours watching "Superman," "The Lone Ranger," or "Lassie" (even animals defend our rights) and not come away with a smug satisfaction that the good guys always win? The television series "The Fugitive," a saga of an unjust manhunt for an innocent man, rewarded our years of faithful viewing with the vindication of the hero and the conviction of the elusive one-armed man. Afterwards we could forget the hard existential reality that an innocent man was made to live as a guilty one for all that time. Admittedly, things have changed on our TV and movie screens, but the Pollyanna world presented by advertising has taken over where they left off. The Yugo, for example, is billed as a car that "anyone can afford." A beer commercial capsulizes this utopian American dream: "Who says you can't have it all?"

Our experience of church life nurtures the seeds of "just desserts spirituality" planted by domestic and cultural mores. Scripture abounds with examples of God's fight for justice on the part of the chosen people, Jesus's preaching and action in favor of justice for the poor, and countless divine promises of the triumph of justice over wrong for those who believe. The preaching of the church has long echoed and reinforced our strong expectations of God to make things right. Finally, popular piety has sometimes raised "false hopes" through the exercise of devotions which emphasize the assurance of divine favors, especially if requested through proper channels like Mary: "Remember, O most gracious Virgin Mary, that never was it known that anyone who fled to thy protection, implored thy help, or sought thy intercession was left unaided." Again, such things are not without their place in the church, but the fact that they have fallen out of the mainstream of pastoral practice indicates that they have been marred by theological imbalance.

Scripture scholarship has helped us mature by informing us of the human element in biblical writings. Assurances of happy endings in Scripture are to some extent human projections onto God of our great desire for more fairness in life, our hope that there must be something better than this, as well as our belief in a God who does redress injustice. All that is as it should be and it certainly doesn't make Christian justice into some kind of naive pipe dream. It does, however, open us to the possibility that such justice does not arrive in the manner and form we might prefer. The experience of life's unfairness forces us beyond piety and preaching which speak of a Hero-God in a white hat who arrives in the nick of time to rescue us from distress. On the other hand, our tradition also rejects potentially fatalistic and passive slogans like "Who said life was fair?" Such sayings suggest that our only recourse is to bite the bullet, that we are powerless to do anything about injustice.

In any case, the key issue here is that we have indeed been promised a rose garden. We have had false hopes in life and unrealistic expectations of God built up through our domestic, cultural, and ecclesial experiences. These lofty ideals have affected our search for justice in a definitive manner. It is now time to back off such claims or at least to redefine them in more realistic, creative, and participatory ways. Our promises of justice may be true, but in what sense are they true?

Admitting Divine Unfairness

The starting point for being ministers of justice in a
messy world is the realization that God is not fair. One
of the Gospel readings that miffs us the most is the
parable of the workers in the vineyard: "Now take your
pay and go home. I want to give this man who was hired
last at much as I gave you. Don't I have the right to do
as I wish with my own money? Or are you jealous
because I am generous? And Jesus concluded, 'So those
who are last will be first, and those who are first will be
last' " (Matt 20/14-16). I would suggest that this passage
bugs us precisely because it is so consistent with human
experience, yet so distant from our hopes and
expectations of God. We end up thinking to ourselves:
"That's how the world is; don't tell me God is that way
too. That couldn't be!"

But, quite frankly, that's exactly how it is according to
this "good news, bad news" story. The good news is that
God is more than fair in a legalistic sense; God is
gracious. The bad news is the "side-effects" of the
Lord's freewheeling approach to giving: all the ways
that God is directly responsible for unfairness in life. A
revealing case is the dispensing of material, physical,
social, and emotional gifts. Anyone can look around and
see quite plainly that God has taken little care to adhere
to that cherished parental custom of dividing the goods
up equally among the children.

There are many examples. A fiscally sound person
wins the lottery while a desperate father gambles away
his unemployment check trying to hit it big. A model

gets rich simply for being born beautiful while a plainer woman "works for a living." A man with several girl friends attracts another just by entering a bar while a shy and lonely one stammers his love life into oblivion. It is true that some balance is built into this divine system, for a blind person does gain in the other senses. Yet, how many blind people, if offered the chance, would trade their keener hearing in a flash for the recovery of their average sight?

God's unjust handling of things can result in major faith crises for the many who have been instructed to expect otherwise. The film *Amadeus* paints a stunning portrait of a man, court composer Salieri, who could not come to terms with God's sloppy and illogical handling of life's treasures: "All I ever wanted was to sing to God. He gave me that longing and then made me mute. Why? Tell me that. If he didn't want me to praise him with music, why implant the desire?" Salieri burns his crucifix and curses the God who could be so cruel as to bless an impious creature like Mozart with unspeakable talents while condemning a faithful servant to mediocrity. How could the love of God (Amadeus) be spoken musically through such an unworthy subject? It was unimagineable, and it spells the end of Salieri's faith: "From now on we are enemies, you and I, because you chose for your instrument a boastful, lustful, smutty, infantile boy and give me for reward only the ability to recognize the incarnation. Because you are unjust, unfair, unkind, I will block you; I swear it."

"Taking Over" for God

Here is a place where we can establish the vital connection between the new ministry's call to "correct God's mistakes" and a specific area of pastoral work like peace and justice. For in the distribution of natural resources on this planet, the Creator has provided everything we need, but has made the "clever error" of doing so disproportionately. So we find "too much" oil in the East, "too much" grain in the West, and so on. God's plan is for us to right such wrongs by redistributing divine gifts according to the needs of the global village rather than hoarding them in a "finders keepers" fashion, allowing the goods to "fall where they may." It's like the world is a jigsaw puzzle for which God has provided all the pieces, but has sent the package "unassembled." Its apparent ugliness at times is a result of this disorder. The task of ministry is to rearrange the pieces, to "put it all together," according to the harmonious design of the Creator.

How can we retain our faith in the God of justice? The minister of justice in life's mess does so by accepting the precarious task of "taking over" for God. Just as the Lord of all gives us stewardship over creation in Genesis, so does the Father of justice send Jesus to call us to participate in justicemaking rather than passively waiting for justice to appear. If there exists a credibility gap regarding God's investment in justice for the poor, we are called as Christians to act according to our "response-abilities" to fill that gap.

This is not an altogether unnatural response to injustice. In fact, when we continue to experience the frustration of injustice, it is quite normal to respond by seeking to make justice happen on our own. There are, however, two ways of going about this task. The first method involves attempting to maintain our share of justice by force, that is, by seeking to "keep things fair" by enforcing a code of justice we rationalize. The second method involves an equally active, but much less violent approach which allows laws to bend precisely for the sake of justice for the poor. Let me clarify these two techniques.

The first method might be referred to as "vigilante justice." When faced with the constant breakdown of laws, either human or divine, which would guarantee our share of justice, we respond by committing ourselves to do what either God or others seem unable or unwilling to do: making things fair! Therefore, this approach does "take over" for God, but in a violent manner which seeks to enforce interiorly felt laws of how things should be. As such, it is a rigid method of justicemaking which does not respond to human experience as much as it denies it. The vigilante justicemaker responds to life with the conviction that: "By God, this life is supposed to be fair and I'm going to force it to be so." God's justice is no longer realized as gift; it is captured as self-righteous plunder.

There are many examples of this type of justicemaking in our messy world. Rambo has become a symbol of forced justice by his cinematic success at winning an unwinnable war and supposedly redeeming the lost pride and honor that is America's heritage. The proliferation of lawsuits in the private sector is also a testimony to this type of justicemaking. Many people who have been mistreated by life now have a way of getting back some of the justice they deserve. They may not be able to get back a son or a leg or a house, but they can sue the daylights out of someone and make big bucks to sooth their misery. Recently a family sued a cemetery because of a freak tragedy in which a tombstone fell over on their young son and killed him. Thus, the loss of a son is cheapened by the illusion that a tidy sum of cash will give purpose to life's accidents. This type of justicemaking is characterized by rigidity, self-centeredness, force, and the drive for immediate retribution.

The Christian Vigilante

The Christian justicemaker in messy times is equally called to take matters into his/her own hands, aware that God's laws do not work (effect justice) on their own. The difference here is that the drive for justice is marked by flexibility rather than rigidity, compassion rather than self-centeredness, responsibility rather than force, acceptance rather than denial, and a desire for ultimate values rather than immediate ones.

Those who seek justice in Jesus are willing to bend the rules for the sake of right because they realize that the suppositions upon which those laws are based are imperfect (e.g., God will send you only what you can handle). Their experience of painful injustice in their own lives opens them up to see and respond to the injustice the world heaps upon the poor rather than redoubled efforts toward acquiring personal rights. The methods employed by such people are marked and guided by the transforming power of love rather than the destructive force of violence. Christian justicemakers struggle to embrace the conditions of life creatively instead of engaging in a neurotic denial of life and obsessive behavior bent upon making it different. Finally, the efforts of these people are focused ahead on the continued transformation of the world rather than on grabbing some transitory value for immediate gratification.

If these ideas arouse suspicion or anxiety, it would be well to recall that participatory justice was rather common in the behavior of Jesus. The Lord was quite comfortable with bending existing laws in specific situations for the sake of a higher priority: "The Law is made for people; people are not made for the Law." Jesus put the law of the Sabbath on hold in order to effect healings and allow his followers to pick corn from the fields for food. He defended this practice before those who were scandalized that he should have the nerve to take the law into his own hands. In word and deed the Lord teaches us that we cannot simply wait around for justice to happen, that we must be instruments of that justice even at the expense of personal popularity or the integrity of individual laws.

The rejection and the acceptance of humanity's share of the burden of justicemaking each have their unique consequences as personified in the stories of two cinematic women. The wages of refusal are paid in the film *Papillon* by an innocent convict who escapes the cruelties of the French penal colony aptly named "Devil's Island." Papillon takes refuge in a convent overnight, hoping to find assistance in his passage to freedom. When he awakes the next morning, prison guards are waiting to recapture him. The convent's superior takes her own sort of refuge from responsibility for turning him in with a tidy summation of how justice works. The nun assures Papillon that his innocence, if genuine, will guarantee him God's protection. It is immediately after she leaves the room that the guards break his foot with a rifle butt and lead him off to many more years of hardship before his eventual escape as an old man. Justice left solely in the hands of God led to protracted injustice.

Our second example, one of a woman who echoes God's cry for justice, comes from a very unlikely source. The movie *The Dead Zone*, based on a Stephen King novel, tells the story of a young man who suffers a tragic form of injustice. At the beginning of the film we witness him saying goodnight to his fiancee during a dangerous storm. Declining her invitation to stay the night, he insists that "some things are worth waiting for." He drives off into the storm only to be involved in a horrible accident which leaves him in a coma. When he awakes he discovers that he has been unconscious for five years and his fiancee, though she waited for a long time, has since met someone else and married.

Later in the film the two of them meet and the stark unfairness of the situation is made evident. The young man tells her: "For you five years have come and gone, but for me it is like the next day." So in time, with the flexibility, compassion, and acceptance of both human and divine limits that mark such hard choices, she offers a gift of Christian justice. Reminding him of his remark that some things are worth waiting for, she asks: "Haven't we waited long enough?" She then makes love with him. Afterwards she is clear about the fact that her gift cannot be repeated because of her marital commitment, but she has nonetheless witnessed something vital from which all Christians can learn. She was God's gift to him and only divine accident, not divine purpose (will), changed that. In the midst of his nightmare she gave him a precious glimpse of the Kingdom dream, a symbol of what was still true in a tidier world, another time and place.

Our sensibilities may incline us toward certain instinctive reactions to this man's dilemma and this woman's response. We may be tempted to rationalize the situation in a number of ways: "God will send him someone else even more special"; "If he accepts his cross, he will merit his crown"; "It's God's will"; "Adultery is wrong and two wrongs do not make a right." Such reasoning, while often containing important bits of truth, must not be allowed to dominate our responses to life's injustice. This is especially true once we are honest enough to admit the scary truth that God does not ensure happy endings in this life without our participation and that pain is not under God's control except through our intervention. The triumph of God's will is usually subject to the discretion of our will in the Spirit. The woman in this story was not being unfaithful to her husband as much as she was restoring God's "lost faithfulness" to an abandoned child.

One of the great obstacles we face in inspiring people to this just endeavor is the mixed messages we send them about the role of their contributions. We spoke previously of the sin of passivity and how it is sometimes fostered in our parishes by the disenfranchisement of people from the operational power of the church. We cannot reinforce our action at the price of people's "passion" on the one hand ("your efforts are superfluous") and expect them to violently shift gears and join the fight for justice and peace on the other ("your efforts are essential"). Such pastoral doubletalk leaves people confused, angry, and withdrawn. More consistency will be demanded before the people of God realize their potential to enflesh the Lord's just dream in the world.

The Justice in Our Hearts

One thing is clear, our tears will continue until ordinary people become convinced that we cannot play life "by the rules" and be assured that justice is being done. Recently a Chicago paper ran a column about a man who purchased a stone from a dealer for a few dollars, knowing full well that it was a very valuable gem. The buyer openly flaunted his new-found wealth, proud of his shrewdness and confident of his innocence insofar as he had clearly obtained it legally or "fairly." We can only imagine the pain of the owner, a man of simple means, at being denied even a token share of the stone's true worth. Insult was added to this injury when the seller was informed that this misfortune (missed fortune) was his own fault. What a sad commentary on a culture that has ensured the reign of injustice for the poor by reinforcing the trustworthiness of rules which benefit the powerful and clever. I was saddened in a parish discussion group by the "matter of fact" assurance with which some defended the legitimacy of this transaction.

Gradually we may discover, as Paul Newman argues in his summation in *The Verdict*, that justice is not in a book (by the book), or in the system, or even in the law. Justice is in our hearts. If we want to have faith in justice, we need only to believe in the power within us and act with justice. Some time ago, after our parish staff had decided to open the sacrament of Eucharist to second grade children, a parishioner complained that the second graders should not be allowed to receive First Communion with the third graders. She argued that her third grader, who had worked three years to prepare for Eucharist, was being unjustly penalized by the admission of children who had labored only two years. We will know when we have reincarnated Gospel justice because our attitudes will reflect the illogical graciousness of the vineyard master rather than the rational and perfect balance of legal proportionality.

Both God and humanity are agents of justice in the world, both have a part to play if righteousness is to prevail. What is God's part? What is our part? These are questions which obviously demand prayerful discernment and constant testing. We realize that we have responsibility to cooperate with God in bringing justice to the world, but where is the line at which this duty ends? One thing is clear: Our response to the world's cry for justice does not begin with a coverup of injustice, but through its revelation. This is the legacy left to us by the great justicemakers of history. Jesus, Gandhi, and Martin Luther King began their efforts to build the Kingdom with strategies which made injustice painfully, embarrassingly evident to those responsible. This is why they were effective; this is why they are were killed. Still, their spirit, the Spirit of God, lives on because they refused to stifle it through private ownership, but "incorporated" it into other people in the knowledge that all are responsible for its power to transform the world into the justice that builds peace.

Items for Individual Reflection/Group Process

1. What has been your experience of injustice in life? Would you agree, in the sense the author intends it, that God has been unfair to you? How would you describe your response to the unfairness of life?

2. Do you have a feeling of responsibility for the making of justice in this life? What are the possibilities and limits of that power?

3. Are you sometimes attracted to what the author refers to as "vigilante justice"? How do you deal with your own inclinations to force justice out of an unfair life experience?

4. Do you agree with the author that there can be a positive and necessary Christian meaning to the idea of "taking matters into you own hands"? Why or why not?

5. How comfortable do you feel with the notion of "bending the rules" for the sake of justice? Do you agree that Jesus did so? Are there boundaries to this practice? What are they? Discuss the actions of justice makers like Gandhi, Martin Luther King, etc. in this regard.

6. Consider the story of the selling of the stone. Do you think the buyer was "within his rights" to buy the gem for a fraction of its worth because of the ignorance of the seller? Why or why not? How would you feel if you owned the stone and this happened to you?

7. How does the parable of the workers in the vineyard strike you? Do you think we could ever successfully sell this philosophy in today's world? Would you want to be part of such a world? Is this parable related to the kind of participatory justice the author is calling for? How?

8. How does competition, as symbolized by America's love affair with sports, influence the ministry of justice in your community? In this country we hate to lose. We idolize and remember winners while scorning and forgetting losers. In what ways do these attitudes undercut the church's ability to serve life's losers, its preference for the poor? In view of the centrality of winning in our culture, how can we communicate a spirituality based on the necessity of losing to win, of being last to be first?

9. How does the rumor mill in your parish block the flow of real justicemaking? What are some ways of lessening the destructive impact of rumors? In what ways do staff members either participate in or challenge this human reality?

Activities for Pastoral Staffs/Ministries

1. Make time both within the pastoral staff and in the community at large to air gripes about unfair policies and practices. Follow up these sessions with specific action plans which address needed change in a sensitive manner. Put these plans on a time line and set a definite date for review/evaluation.

2. "Secular realities" like professional sports strikes reveal how reluctant people are to "take the ball in their own hands" and real-ize their power to change things. Despite endless complaints about player strikes, no one has ever organized a fan strike. On the contrary, when the players return, so do the paying fans. Identify the issues in your community that get people upset. How can they be invited to participate in change rather than talk?

3. Children are often most subject to the influence of Hollywood stereotypes of justice because of the vast amount of television they view. Initiate a campaign to limit television or a program of family discussion which would contrast popular television and film heroes with Christian justicemakers as represented in a film like *Gandhi*.

4. Pastors, staff, and other pastoral leaders might analyze their methods of conflict management. Is there a tendency to let "sleeping dogs lie" (which leads to gossip), to reassert control (which leads to anger and disengagement), or to negotiate and compromise (which leads to justice and peace)? Study recent conflicts in the community along with the manner in which they were resolved. Attend to their lessons and make adjustments.

5. Tape some commercials and view them as a group. How do these advertisements influence our practice of justice? Do we shrug them off or do they affect us in sutble ways? Identify some of the ads that may help to perpetuate an unjust world by the illusions they create about life. One surprising example is the current Disney ad campaign which implies that only life's winners (of

Super Bowls and Olympic gold) merit an invitation to "the Magic Kingdom." Devise ways of combatting these illusions through a ministry of peace and justice. Do we ever tend to commercialize God or the church? How?

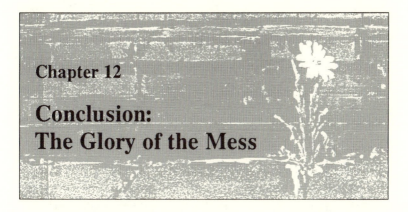

Chapter 12

Conclusion:
The Glory of the Mess

"His blindness has nothing to do with his sins or his parents'. He is blind so that God's power might be seen at work in him."
— John 9/3

Early in the film *The Natural* the stage is set for Roy Hobb's meteoric rise to the level of mythic hero. Like tales of historic champions born of noblest lineage, his story exudes the promise of which legends are made. Born and raised amid the simple grace of farm life, possessed of amazing athletic gifts, and armed with "wonder boy," a bat carved from the wood of a tree split by lightning, he is summoned to Chicago by the Cubs. Roy Hobbs is to be given a chance to fulfill his childhood dream of playing major league baseball, indeed, of being the best baseball player who ever played the game.

On the way to Chicago, Hobbs demonstrates that there is no doubt as to the outcome of his tryout. A chance encounter with baseball's famed player, "The Whammer," allows him to showcase his abilities. On a bet by his manager he strikes out the game's greatest hitter on three straight pitches. Clearly, all that remains is for Hobbs to show up in Chicago and play out the scenario his marvelous beginnings foreshadow. Perched on the brink of a fairy tale existence, Hobbs receives a phone call from a mysterious woman whom he met on the train. Invited to her hotel room, he enters to find her ominously dressed in black. She asks him if he is truly going to be the best baseball player ever to play the game. As soon as Hobbs affirms this she raises a gun and shoots him, shattering the fairy tale that seemed so inevitable. It is sixteen years later before Roy Hobbs gets another shot at glory.

This may seem like an odd way to begin a chapter dedicated to expounding the glories of a messy world, but I do so purposely to face the challenge of illustrating my point with a difficult case. If this life is truly glorious and hopeful, then it must prove to be so in even the darkest of times, the strangest of circumstances. When Roy Hobbs returns to Chicago after a sixteen year absence he offers a blunt answer to his boyhood sweetheart's inquiry about what happened: "My life didn't turn out the way I expected." My concern as we conclude this reflection on ministry in a messy world is that we grasp and value this most universal human experience, that people's lives don't turn out the way they expect, as an opening to doing ministry. I would like to spend some time exploring those characteristics which make our mess valuable, vital, and even glorious for all ministry.

The Mess as Normal and Inevitable

The first step toward making the mess a positive element in ministry rather than an obstacle is the realization that a messy world is quite normal; it is our home. This admission saves us from the considerable frustration and useless turmoil that arises when we attempt to rid ourselves of messiness, wish it away, or get around it. When we begin to feel at home with our mess and its consequences, we have a lot more resources in reserve for caring. This energy might previously have been expended upon efforts to change the ground rules or the scenario for ministry.

This may be what Jesus had in mind when he lashed out at Peter for suggesting that he avoid the messiness of his coming passion and death: "Get away from me, Satan! You are an obstacle in my way, because these thoughts of yours don't come from God, but from humankind." The Lord's disciples were constantly urging him to stop fooling around and "clean up the town." One tendency that Christians could be consistently convicted of might be this reluctance to embrace the truth that the path to real glory winds through the thicket of suffering and death. Yet, we accept the mess, not as an end in itself, but as a starting point and backdrop for all our pastoral efforts. This change in viewpoint is subtle, but naming a messy world as normal and inevitable allows us to focus our energies on aiding people to live creatively within its boundaries rather than on planning constant "escape attempts" and puzzling over the repeated failure of such plans.

Anyone who lives in Chicago is well aware of two realities:

1. In the winter it is difficult to travel because the weather often clogs up the expressways.

2. In the summer it is difficult to travel because crews are constantly fixing the roads after the wear and tear of winter.

What Chicago resident has not implored the gods for one season of reprieve from inclement weather or road repair? Eventually, though, Chicagoans resign themselves to the inevitability of road hazards and learn to travel despite them. So it is that the temptation of the spiritual life is to seek a dispensation from "road hazards" for the best of intentions: "God, if only you would remove this obstacle from my life, I could really go somewhere, I would work wonders for you." The challenge of the journey is to accept God's preference for making us "stunt drivers," resourceful travelers, on the obstacle course of life.

The Mess as the Starting Point for Ministry

There is no ministry without the mess. Those engaged in pastoral work can give thanks to God for creating such a flawed existence, for making so many "mistakes." In a more perfect world professional ministers would be the victims of planned obsolescence and our caring for each other would be reduced to superfluous gameplaying. Ministers in a messy world are much more than props in a cosmic magic show, participants in a divine "slight of hand." We disciples are invited to enflesh divine power in our very weakness, to be so needed by the Lord that God's people will not be loved and cherished without us. A simple example of this truth is the powerlessness of a phrase like "Smile, God loves you!" without the intervention of human love to validate that claim.

Skepticism about messiness as a starting point for ministry is certainly not new. In scripture Nathanael questions Jesus's Messianic credentials on the basis of his shady background: "Can anything good come from Nazareth?" John Shea, in his book *An Experience Named Spirit*, points out one origin of this problem. The apostles, he explains, first witnessed the humanity of Jesus and then saw God's glory emerge out of that limitedness. Because of Scripture we share the "disadvantage" of having the divinity of Jesus as a starting point; we know something they didn't know. So, our struggle is to discover Christ's humanity, to embrace the Incarnation as an asset rather than a liability to the Messianic mission. Throughout history there have arisen heresies which try to deny the "scandal" of the Lord's humanity on the basis of the implausibility that a wretched human could ever embody divinity.

We grew up safe and secure in the faith that the world was firmly under God's control and that any troubles we encountered were the result of carefully planned divine tests. That sense of security gave rise to pastoral images which found expression in our culture. Bing Crosby became our ministerial hero in films like *Going My Way* and *The Bells of St. Mary's*. His calm and reassuring presence, symbolized by his pipe, both spoke and fed our belief that the tranquil world of the parish church and school was the center of all life. Small crises might arise, but with a token intervention by our benevolent hero things would certainly "return to normal." It never bothered us that Crosby didn't do much because our faith hinged on the conviction that not much needed doing. He was the personification of a ministry that was a comforting luxury, frosting on the cake recipe of the Lord's pastoral plan for us.

Contrast this pastoral image with the modern sense of desperation that gives rise to such a cry for relief that the chasm between human ministry and the efficacy of God's love is bridged. Mother Theresa's ministry reaches its apex as she stares into the face of death. Here is a soul who has accepted the messiness of life and humbly embraced God's desperate need of her to offer a moment of reassuring comfort to the dying. Bishop Hunthausen of Seattle refused easy denials of our messy world and chose instead to reach out to those who don't fit existing pastoral categories. As a result he was made to stand as outcast with the people who benefited from his work. These are our ministerial mentors for these messy times. Their lives are not couched in serenity and their days are not played out amid artificial or cute crises. The grittiness of their ministries is the crux of the hope they hold out to the world. Such ministers plunge their hands into the muddy waters of life and uncover a pool of light that has the power to bathe us all in the glory of the Lord.

The Mess as a Fountain of Glory

Messiness is the fountain from which the beauty and glory of human existence flows. Without the mess, moments of authentic triumph in life would be impossible. While this sounds absurd from a certain point of view, reflecting back upon the stories that have inspired us and kept us going through the tough times reveals how true a statement it is. If any of us were to name those stories which are most important to us, the ones we remember and hold in our hearts for the journey, I would wager that the main thing they hold in common is their symbolism of human victory in the face of overwhelming obstacles. We may question a plot device in a film or book because it seems forced, it does not fit. We sit in the theatre or chair and ask: "Why did that have to happen?" The answer to our question is painfully simple: If "that" didn't happen there would be no story and no glory. The book or movie would end immediately for lack of conflict.

It is this dramatic conflict which gives stories significance and provides them with their power for personal transformation. Imagine the great stories of history without conflict. Picture the couple in O. Henry's "Gift of the Magi" as Yuppies with Mastercards and their sacrificial giving becomes superfluous. Would the love between Romeo and Juliet be nearly as memorable if it were not tragically contrasted by the destructive hatred between the Montagues and Capulets? Rewrite the *Star Wars* saga without Darth Vader and it becomes a rather forgettable endeavor. Realize that the triumph of the Resurrection loses much of its transforming power if the presence of the cross is softened or deleted. Many modern movies sacrifice the mythic power of human struggle for the popular illusion of invulnerability (I cannot die) and solitariness (I can do it alone). Invincible loners may sell tickets, but it is the triumph of the vulnerable in solidarity that forges human hearts for the journey.

Jesus constantly hammered home this same point. He reminded us that without death there is no life, without letting go there is no holding on, without losing there is no winning, and without being last there is no being first. In contemporary language we might phrase the Lord's wisdom in other ways: It is good villains which make good heroes, tragic beginnings which set the stage for happy endings, heartbreak which paves the way to true love, and the gloom of night which announces the glory of the new day. Without our messes we might well have a lot more fun and relaxation, but our moments of redemptive glory would be few and far between. The memories which form our self image and carry us through life are those which involve gaining a prize at the cost of great personal loss or suffering. When we come face to face with God it will be such triumphs in the face of the cross that will mark us as the Lord's.

The Mess as the Impetus and Hallmark of Holiness

Author Gail Sheehy uses the term "life accident" to describe those experiences which challenge our expectations of God and human existence. The importance of such events is that they take us aback and cause us to reassess our situation and the direction of our life. These occurrences then become the potential springboards to conversion, a process of turning around toward a new, more lifegiving direction. Like the experience of running into a wall, these moments shake our confidence and our sense of balance. They often make us "patients" for a time and afford us the luxury of review and replanning. More than anything else, however, these times are valuable because without them we might continue on the paths of least resistance without asking the necessary questions or undertaking the vital reassessment.

So it is that messiness is the impetus for change in our spiritual lives. Those whose lives are messy are constantly urged by their life circumstances to take a look around for something better, more satisfying. Jesus was most comfortable in the company of such people because his own life was about the call to dynamic conversion over passive self-satisfaction. The one group that was continually on Jesus's "hit list" was the Pharisees, individuals whose authority and power allowed them to rest in their self-righteousness and control over life. Such persons, Jesus criticized, look neat on the outside but are actually among the most messy, "full of dead men's bones." The drive toward holiness is fueled by the dis-ease of an unordered life.

Messiness is not only the impetus toward creative change, it is its hallmark. Those whose lives are disorderly (disjointed, disintegrated) are also most likely to be numbered among the holy (whole, integrated). Nowhere was this startling paradox more forcefully announced by Jesus than in the Beatitudes. Many of the Beatitudes associate the life of blessedness, even happiness, with messiness and disorder: "Blessed are the poor; blessed are those who mourn; blessed are those who hunger and thirst; blessed are the persecuted." Poverty and brokenness are the hallmarks of the whole (holy) life.

Control and order, on the other hand, are the badges of those in danger of losing their way on the road to holiness: "Woe to you rich, for you have had your easy life; Woe to you who are full now, for you shall go hungry; Woe to you who laugh now, for you shall mourn and weep; Woe to you when all people speak well of you; their ancestors said the same thing about the false prophets." So, it seems that when the divine physician is taking the vital signs of his followers, it is much happier for us if we are in the company of those diagnosed as diseased rather than healthy and whole.

The Mess Is Vital
for True Growth and Development

Apparent and temporary growth is the product of ministry based upon control and order. The church is learning, though, that authentic and lasting growth is the result of the willingness to minister in the midst of a messy world. Let us examine three simple examples of this movement in the pastoral vision of the ecclesial community.

1. Enablement is taking the place of "I'm-ablement" as a ministerial priority. Instead of providing the people of God with bread and feeding them for a day we are realizing the wisdom of teaching them to grow their own grain and feeding them for a lifetime. Similarly, Eucharistic theology no longer emphasizes "receiving communion" as an isolated value but includes the corresponding demand of helping people to become the Body of Christ for one another. The primary task of the pastoral minister is to discern and activate the gifts of the community for the service of the church. This demands new skills, in particular, the willingness to let go of being in charge.

Possibly the hardest thing about learning to let go is the knowledge that things might initially run more efficiently if the minister were to remain in charge. Assuming the task of enablement as a priority requires that we divert our attention from the initial mess we will create, and our gut instinct to jump in and clean up, while looking down the road to the eventual proficiency of the people we empower. This skill demands of us that we focus on the truth that ministry is not ours to own but ours to give away. The strange logic of this commitment is that messy ministry in the hands of God's people is preferable to orderly ministry solely in the alien hands of the professional.

2. Diversity within the pastoral community is here to stay and challenges us to respond creatively to its messiness. It is an alluring temptation for all of us to sanction a small band of remote leaders and accept the luxury of their exclusive proclamation of the vision of the community. Yet, openness to the Spirit which "blows where it will" must eventually challenge us to forge new and less tidy models of our pastoral life that recognize and celebrate our diversity. James and Evelyn Whitehead's book, *The Emerging Laity*, addresses this call: "When we restrict the sense of the faithful to a universal and rhetorical level, we avoid these messy problems. But if we accept the reality of 'the sense of the faithful' in the practical life of the community of faith, we must confront our diversity."

Uniformity is comforting and tidy, while diversity is challenging and messy. Yet, the consolation of uniformity is illusory and short-lived, giving the impression of a house united and forging onward. In reality, an oppressive commitment to uniformity has historically led to periods of intellectual and spiritual stagnation in the church (a point made by Archbishop Weakland of Milwaukee in response to the dismissal of Charles Curran from his teaching post at Catholic University). The cost of such stagnation for the sake of order may be high. Are we willing to sacrifice the ideas, dreams, imaginations, enthusiasm, questions, and commitment of those with whom we differ for the sake of order and clarity? The mess created by the loss of those gifts may be much more than that averted. The power and richness of our diversity, on the other hand, like a tapestry whose diverse and intricate weave graces a community with beauty and strength, is a gift well worth the sacrifice it demands of us.

3. We are learning that the sharing of power rather than the exercise of power over others is the messier but more authentic means of energizing the faith community: "Earthly kings lord it over their people. Those who exercise authority over them are called their benefactors. Yet, it cannot be that way with you. Let the greater among you be as the junior, the leader as the servant" (Luke 22/25-26).

Once again, the Whiteheads' book, *The Emerging Laity*, captures this shift in our perception of the manner in which power is efficacious. Power, they suggest, is becoming appreciated as a relational dynamic of the faith community rather than as a possession of a select group of leaders. The community, in fact, as a product of that power, authorizes its use for the good of everyone and participates intimately in its dynamics. A model of leadership, then, which is out of touch with the community and its needs relinquishes its claim to authority. This emerging sense of power as a relational dynamic authorized and utilized by the faith community is much more ambiguous and messy, but ultimately more fulfilling and effective.

The church is no different than any modern day institution. The faith community runs on energy and is under the influence of the "energy crises" which are so common in the world today. We are challenged to steward our existing energies even as we risk the search for new ones. Unlike energy companies which must conduct exhausting tests to verify the worth of newly discovered energy sources, the people of God share with church hierarchy the priceless and true energy of God's Spirit. Once we are willing to transcend our fears about potential pastoral disasters, we have at our disposal stores of untapped power in the "ordinary people" with whom the Lord is patiently dwelling in the hope of being released for the transformation of the world according to God's ancient dream.

Ministry Means "Working in the Dark"

I was part of a staff meeting recently where the topic of the Holy Week Triduum schedule came up. The pastor, looking for continuity and better attendance, promoted the idea of holding the Easter Vigil an hour earlier. The associate and I pointed out that it would still be daylight at that hour and the light service would surely be rendered ineffective. This argument did not win out, however, and the Vigil was scheduled to begin in the daylight.

The symbolic weight of this incident for making the point of these pages is considerable. The liturgy speaks its wisdom quite plainly that Easter Vigil cannot be celebrated during the day because light cannot appear out of light, but only out of darkness. In the language employed earlier, we might say that the glory of the light is more apparent against the darkness. As liturgists we know this truth, but we forget or ignore it for the sake of convenience or practicality. So too, as ministers we realize that life comes most gracefully out of death, hope out of despair, love out of loneliness, and calm out of the storm, but we lose this truth and continue to pattern our ministry according to more tidy models. One can only marvel at and anticipate the pastoral future that awaits us when we fully embrace the wisdom of the liturgy by refusing to "schedule our ministry in the daylight." Instead, our pastoral work will unfold in the darkness of life so that the light it sheds upon the world will be accessible to everyone in the house.

So, we might return to the ending of *The Natural* to see how our hero, Roy Hobbs, is doing. Sixteen years after his initial setback he is standing at the plate with a shot at fulfilling his lifelong dream of baseball glory. He has secured his chance to be a hero, to win the pennant for a downtrodden bunch of losers. We might ask why it is necessary for him to play under the threat of blackmail, to bleed from that old gunshot wound, to learn that his pitcher is in cahoots with the bad guys, to break his trusty homemade bat, to trail by two runs, and to be down two strikes with two out in the bottom of the ninth. After all, hasn't he been through enough? In one sense the answer to these questions is quite complex and elusive, but in another it is rather simple. The greater the odds against you and the more obstacles to be overcome, the more clear and inspiring is the divine power and glory revealed in ultimate victory. This is why the myth is a cornerstone of the power to minister.

Yet, in Hollywood there is always the luxury of changing the ending to suit the audience's fancy. In Malamud's novel, *The Natural*, Hobbs strikes out at the end. Producers hold special screenings of their films prior to nationwide distribution just so they can gauge the film's popularity. If the ending is poorly received, a new one will be filmed. In real life we do not have such a luxury. Long ago Jesus prayed in the Garden and begged the Father for a different ending to his story. The Father's refusal to edit the script resulted in passion and death, but also in the glory of the Resurrection. As disciples of the Lord it is our calling to embrace the messiness of life so that the glory of the Lord may shine for all to see. As Jesus reminded his distraught followers on the road to Emmaus: "Was it not necessary that the Messiah should suffer these things and so enter into his glory?"

Items for Individual Reflection/Group Process

1. Is the messiness and ambiguity of life essential to the manifestation of God's glory in life? Can God's glory be revealed just as plainly in cleaner ways? How?

2. Do you believe that your life, or life in general, will have a "happy ending"? What are the dimensions of such happiness? What do you expect a happy ending to look like?

3. Do you feel "normal" when your life is messy? How do we get to the point where we appreciate the "blessing" of conflict and ambiguity? Is this possible?

4. Reflect upon the times when you have been of greatest help to another. How do you feel about your part in that situation? What was it was about your role that made you truly helpful rather than a token presence? Did you make the problem go away or was your success founded on a different premise?

5. How have your struggles made you holier? Name some of your virtues that have developed directly through the challenges of hardship.

6. Do you find it difficult as a minister to let go of your area of control so that someone else can learn by making a mess of it? How do we acquire that ability? Who allowed you to learn ministry by letting you mess up their domain?

7. Do you accept diversity as the status quo for the pastoral community? Are there ways in which you are tempted to seek uniformity? What are they? How do you avoid them?

8. John Steinbeck once said that the greatest danger facing America is success. How could we apply this statement to the church and to pastoral ministry in view of the ideas expressed in this book?

9. How do people retain their human dignity, their likeness to God, amid life's most desperate circumstances? Case studies can be found by contrasting the film *Lord of the Flies* with *Empire of the Sun* or *Sophie's Choice* with *The Miracle Worker*. What are the graces that allow people to triumph in such circumstances? What are the realities that overwhelm them? How can the triumphs of grace be maximized and its failures be minimized? The film *Runaway Train* is also a poignant, but disturbing, reflection on this difficult question.

Activities for Pastoral Staffs/Ministries

1. Identify the top two or three crises that your community or group has experienced over the past few years. Name the glories that arose from facing them. If no benefits can be identified, seek out the reasons and determine if there is a need for change in your style of crisis management.

2. Assess the degree of willingness in your staff or ministry to welcome the sharing of authority (ie. take the risk that less capable newcomers will foul up your work while assuming it). What concrete steps can be taken to facilitate needed letting go, the incorporation of new members, and the transfer of the rightful ownership of ministry into the hands of people?

3. List the strengths and weaknesses of your group or ministry as a whole. Name how they complement each other and how they are dependant upon each other (e.g., my passivity means that I sometimes am not assertive, but it reaps benefits in receptivity to others). What are the strengths of your weaknesses, the weaknesses of your strengths?

4. Collegiality is here to stay as a much less tidy model of pastoral leadership. Yet, church leaders cling to the old ways by retaining "final say" over pastoral decisions. Is "last word" authority still operative in your ministry? Is it effective? Is it impossible to do without? Discuss the story of Solomon's judgement (1 Kings 3/16-28). Is Solomon's offer to cut the child in two similar to the way we parcel out authority into pieces so that we can retain ownership and control over parishes, projects, or ideas that we view as "our baby"? Do we actually cut the life out of our ministry by doing so? Who is "the real mother" of our pastoral life?

5. Do a wrap-up assessment of this book with regard to its meaning for your ministry, staff, or community. Consider how the book

might be used in other facets of your parish or community. Develop a followup plan that will ensure that whatever insights were gained on ministry are concretized in action plans.